WHAT PEOPLE ARE SAYING

I met with Dan Bolin once a month when I first became a camp director. I had already been a part of camp life for a decade and still had a lot to learn. His mentoring helped tremendously and am so thankful for many of his teachings in book form! Outlining the 10 Principles of Camp Ministry is a biblical master class on many aspects to being a camp leader.
Paul Biles
Executive Director, Tejas Camp & Retreats, Texas

Jesus: Camp Director is an insightful and refreshing perspective on the unique and powerful experience of Christian camping. Bolin's years of leadership in camping is evident as he outlines the wholistic nature of Christ's ministry to his "staff" and to his "campers". The principles of ministry outlined in this book are clear and effective. Everyone in camping leadership can benefit from this book!
Brent Bounds, Ph.D.
Clinical Psychologist, New York

No one embodies Christian Camping like my former colleague and current friend, Dan Bolin. His keen understanding and experience of the life-changing work of camping ministry and his love for God's Word meet in the creative example of Jesus, the 5,000, and the thousands of campers and staff Dan has influenced as a leader over five decades of faithful service. Dive into *Jesus: Camp Director* and be grounded, encouraged, and inspired.
Dr. April L. Moreton
Executive Director of Advancement Evangelical Alliance Mission, Minnesota

This was an absolutely delightful read! Thank you. I thoroughly enjoyed it and found myself motivated in ministry. The ideas are insightful and the applications to camp ministry are made with graceful impact.
Dr. Wayne Braudrick
Lead Pastor, Frisco Bible Church, Texas

Dan Bolin has a demonstrated passion for coming along side of young learning camp directors and also seasoned older camp ministry staff, clearly communicating through his experience and scripture the Biblical principles of servant leadership. *Jesus: Camp Director*, is a book you should read as you begin your ministry in camping and also a book I have enjoyed and learned from as a lifelong seasoned veteran of the camping ministry.
David 'Twig' Hartwig
Director, Faith Bible Camp, Illinois

Dr. Dan Bolin has been known for bringing biblical principles to camp ministry, and this book is no exception. It is incredible how he uncovers the secrets of the Feeding of the 5,000 and translates them into applications in our daily ministerial and personal lives. This book opens new perspectives on the best camp director of all time. Jesus!
Evelyn Rivas de Umaña
Executive Director, Christian Camping Latin America

Camp directors learn about these principles quickly when faced with the responsibilities of running camp. How much easier it would have been to have read this book before I started my journey as a camp director - Many of these I learned the hard way. Thanks Dan, for clearly outlining how Jesus handled them.
Ross Bay
New Zealand

The feeding of the 5,000 offers a window into how Jesus approached ministry. This quick read is packed with helpful insights and valuable gems for the Christian camping professional, or about anyone in ministry.
Dathan Brown
Former Executive Director - Hume Lake Christian Camps, California

Dan Bolin is masterful at drawing parallels between the things we do every day and how that fits into spiritual truths. Dan brings the miracle of feeding the 5,000 to life as he explores what Jesus did with and for his disciples and relates it to camp ministry today. Ten principles that are applicable and practical. A great read for every person in camp leadership!
Sharon Fraess
National Director, CCI/Canada

In his book, **Jesus: Camp Director,** Dan Bolin beautifully and effectively captures the heart of Jesus and applies it to camp ministry. If only I had this book at the beginning of my 25 years in Christian camping! I highly recommend those leading Christian camps, or virtually any Christian ministry, not only read this book, but also use it as a staff training resource.
Sue Nigh
Heartland Conference Retreat Center, Ohio

JESUS: CAMP DIRECTOR

© 2023 Dan Bolin | Refueling in Flight Ministries, Inc

All rights reserved. No part of this book may be reproduced or used in any manner without the prior written permission of the copyright owner, except for the use of brief quotations in a book review. To request permissions, contact the publisher at info@refuelinginflight.com.

Hardcover: 979-8-9850725-5-6
Paperback: 979-8-9850725-3-2
E-book: 979-8-9850725-6-3
Library of Congress Control Number: 2023921019

RIF Publishing
PO Box 3115
Arlington, VA 22203
www.refuelinginflight.com
First Edition | Arlington VA | 2023

Scripture References
Taken from The Holy Bible, New International Version® NIV® Copyright © 1973 1978 1984 2011 by Biblica, Inc. TM Used by permission. All rights reserved worldwide.

Names: Bolin, Dan, author. | McDowell, Ed, foreword by.
Title: Jesus: Camp Director
Subtitle: 5,000 Campers, 12 Interns and 0 Kitchen Staff

JESUS: CAMP DIRECTOR

5,000 Campers
12 Interns
0 Kitchen Staff

WRITTEN BY
DR. DAN BOLIN

FOREWORD BY ED MCDOWELL

To Dan DeGroat

Whose godly example, wise counsel, professional expertise, and warm friendship has influenced Christian camping around the world.

*In many ways, the stunning miracle of the Feeding of the 5,000 and the events leading up to it, created a context much like today's Christian camps, and Jesus proved to be the **expert camp director**.*

Dr. Dan Bolin

CONTENTS

FOREWORD 17
INTRODUCTION 21
CHAPTER ONE 29
    The Principle of Intentionality
CHAPTER TWO 43
    The Principle of Holistic Engagement
CHAPTER THREE 53
    The Principle of Inability
CHAPTER FOUR 63
    The Principle of Green-Grass
CHAPTER FIVE 77
    The Principle of Chewable Bites
CHAPTER SIX 89
    The Principle of Gratitude
CHAPTER SEVEN 101
    The Principle of Strategic Programming
CHAPTER EIGHT 113
    The Principle of Stewardship
CHAPTER NINE 127
    The Principle of Dual Impact
CHAPTER TEN 137
    The Principle of the Big Body
EPILOGUE 149
    ENDNOTES 150
    ACKNOWLEDGEMENTS 153
    ABOUT THE AUTHOR 157
    OTHER BOOKS BY THE AUTHOR 159
    ABOUT REFUELING IN FLIGHT MINISTRIES 160
    ABOUT ED MCDOWELL 161

FOREWORD

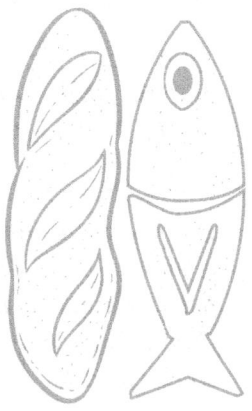

In his sequel to *Blueprints*, author Dan Bolin provides a compelling connection between Jesus and the work of being in Christian camping. He identifies ten specific principles that move from *why* we are doing what we do (***Blueprints***) to *how* we go about doing it (***Jesus: Camp Director.***)

Dan draws heavily from the story of the Feeding of the 5,000 as told in all four gospels. Here is Luke's account of it:

> *When the apostles returned, they reported to Jesus what they had done. Then he took them with him and they withdrew by themselves to a town called Bethsaida, but the crowds learned about it and followed him.*
>
> *He welcomed them and spoke to them about the kingdom of God, and healed those who needed healing.*
>
> *Late in the afternoon the Twelve came to him and said, "Send the crowd away so they can go to the surrounding villages and countryside and find food and lodging, because we are in a remote place here."*
>
> *He replied, "You give them something to eat."*

They answered, "We have only five loaves of bread and two fish—unless we go and buy food for all this crowd." (About five thousand men were there.)

But he said to his disciples, "Have them sit down in groups of about fifty each." The disciples did so, and everyone sat down. Taking the five loaves and the two fish and looking up to heaven, he gave thanks and broke them. Then he gave them to the disciples to distribute to the people.

They all ate and were satisfied, and the disciples picked up twelve basketfuls of broken pieces that were left over. (Luke 9:10-17)

Reflection

As I read through the ten principles, there was a clear application for each one in the camping ministry I serve as Executive Director. *Principle of the Green-Grass* (Chapter Four) stood out to me, in large part because of what my father, Bob McDowell (1930-2023), a lifelong champion for Christian camping, taught me:

> *It's not about what you don't have that accomplishes powerful ministry in God's Kingdom. It is about what you do have and what God does with it that matters.*
> - Bob McDowell

Dan Bolin explains this principle as *"Doing our Best"* in whatever context our camp operates. He knows this firsthand. His leadership roles in Christian camping around the world have seen God work in amazing ways through Christian camps, ranging from the humblest of settings to highly developed properties and programs.

As camp directors, we can fret over what we do not have, and lose sight of the opportunities right in front of us. At times, we look at other camps and fall prey to the adage *"the grass is greener on the other side."*

The Principle of the Green-Grass focuses on doing our best in the setting God has provided for us right now. Dan goes on to say that building trust and minimizing distractions are possible in any setting with a commitment to meeting the practical needs of people and creatively drawing the most out of the space available to work with. God will multiply the impact of this humble and faithful effort in ways that encourage our faith and challenge our imagination.

Encouragement

If Christian camp directors take time to read, discuss with their teams, and put into practice the principles of *Jesus: Camp Director*, the impact could be significant. Applying these principles could draw hundreds of thousands of people, if not millions, to Christ through Christian camping and bring them into a life-changing relationship with Jesus Christ.

It will be because we are doing the best with what we have, building trust by meeting needs, and minimizing distractions so that the path is clear to the cross of Jesus Christ for everyone coming to camp.

Prayer

Dear Jesus,

Thank You for leading Dan Bolin to write *Jesus: Camp Director* based on the practical application of Your truth, as modeled in the *Feeding of the 5,000*.

Thank You for giving everyone in Christian camping ten clear principles that focus on how to do Christian camping in a way that draws people to You.

Please help leaders and teams in Christian camping take up the opportunity to apply these principles.

We trust You with the increase this will bring into the Kingdom of God, knowing in faith, that it will be far more than 5,000 people and 12 baskets of leftovers.

Together, in Your name Jesus, we pray,

Amen

Ed McDowell
Executive Director
Warm Beach Camp Ministries
October 2023

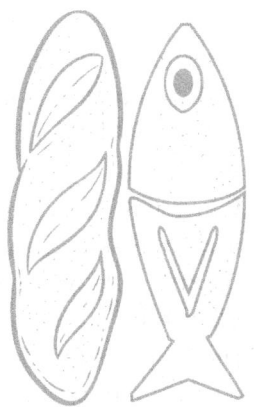

INTRODUCTION

My earlier book, **Blueprints**, addresses the biblical foundations for Christian camping and attempts to answer the critical question *'why?'* That is where we always start; we must have a solid biblical basis for what we do in ministry – and life. But we also need to answer the question, *'how?'* This book, ***Jesus: Camp Director***, explores ten principles Jesus used to accomplish the ministry set before him. We enhance our ministry effectiveness as we replicate *how* Jesus ministered during one of his most astounding earthly encounters.

Jesus was an amazing camp director. He masterfully applied these ten timeless and universal principles in a camp-like setting. He provided a powerful example for how camping leaders can do ministry today. And these ten foundational methods can be applied well beyond camps to enhance any ministry context.

I'm a camp guy. I spent my teenage years volunteering in wilderness adventure camps and my college years on summer staff at a residential camp. I've cleaned a lot of toilets, swimming pools, and dirty dishes. And I've served as CEO of Pine Cove, chaired the board of Christian Camp and Conference Association, and spent 10-years as international director of Christian Camping International. From that point of view, it is easy for me to see the application of these principles to the Christian camping world. However, I've also been around a broad assortment of Christian churches and organizations. I briefly worked on a church staff during my days in seminary. My wife served on the staff of a local church for almost 10 years. I ran a Christian radio station for nine years, and I've served on the boards of mission agencies and educational institutions. The principles that Jesus employed are expressed well in the world of Christian camping, but also apply to other ministries. They are timeless and universal.

These ten principles are not the only elements that comprise powerful ministries, but these ten should be considered and applied in every ministry context. They are not the 'end all' in ministry design, but they provide a good place to start.

The Feeding of the 5,000 stands alone as the only miracle (besides the resurrection) recorded in all four Gospels. In a remote setting, at an inconvenient time, Jesus displayed his power over the ordinary limits of physics, the meager resources of rural Palestine, and the selfish desires of human hearts.

> *A short staff retreat was just what they all needed.*

For the disciples, the Feeding of the 5,000 followed a busy and tiring ministry season. They had actively engaged in healing, miracles, teaching, and spiritual warfare. They were exhausted, yet excited. They needed a chance to unwind, debrief, and process what they had just experienced. A break was in order and that was the plan; a short staff retreat was just what they all needed. But as often happens

INTRODUCTION

in life, things didn't work out as expected. Jesus jettisoned his plans for the disciples' scheduled get-away and engaged 5,000 *campers* who arrived unexpectedly.

In many ways, this stunning miracle and the events leading up to it, created a context much like today's Christian camps, and Jesus proved to be the expert camp director. Christian camping leaders today can learn many practical and powerful principles for camp ministry from Jesus' example. How he met the challenges of his day and how he used this camp-like experience provides ten illustrative patterns for how we might lead our camps today.

Jesus met the people's physical and spiritual needs. He enlisted Interns (his disciples) to accomplish the work. He organized the campers into small groups and employed a variety of ministry styles to accomplish his purposes. He used this engagement to not only meet the needs of the 5,000 campers, but he also strategically invested in his disciples to strengthen and train them throughout their time as *staff members*.

Each of the Gospel writers describe the story in slightly different ways, emphasizing various aspects and contributing unique details. As usual, Matthew, Mark, and Luke share many common recollections while John's account is the most unique. Together these four perspectives provide a fascinating window into how Jesus did ministry. More to the point of this study, they reveal how Jesus might have functioned as a modern-day camp director.

Specifically, this short book looks at ten ministry principles that shaped how Jesus interacted with the people he cared for. Not surprisingly, this miracle took place outside; over half of Jesus' recorded teaching occurred in outdoor settings, 16% indoors and 33% in undisclosed settings.[1] These ministry principles work anywhere, but they certainly work well in the heart of God's magnificent creation.

Each chapter provides a window into one of these *Ten Principles of Camp Ministry*.

The first is the *Principle of Intentionality*: Ministry opportunities constantly come our way. We face a never-ending series of choices regarding how to serve and lead. We can easily become distracted and our efforts diffused, leading to strenuous activity but void of focus and effectiveness. Purpose, plans, and priorities help us determine the best way to engage the fluid circumstances of our world. Jesus masterfully focused on his purpose, set his plans, and adjusted his ministry activity to accommodate the changing circumstances he encountered.

Second, is the *Principle of Holistic Engagement*: Camp is uniquely positioned to minister to real people with complex needs. People hurt physically and spiritually, and these pains often flow from emotional trauma and broken relationships. Christian camp leaders are called to minister to whole people, those with deep and complicated sources of pain, just like Jesus did. Camp is a great place to engage every aspect of a person's life.

Third, Jesus revealed to his disciples the *Principle of Inability*: No one is ever ready for ministry challenges—and if they think they are, then quite probably they are not. Jesus' disciples were expected to meet the needs of a massive throng of people. Many were sick, injured, and infirmed, but everyone was waiting and hoping for the long-promised Messiah. The people faced overwhelming physical and spiritual needs and the disciples were ill-prepared to respond.

Fourth, Jesus exemplified the *Principle of the Green-Grass*. By *green-grass*, I mean, *providing our best*. Jesus didn't have much to work with, but he told the people to sit down in the green grass, not in the dirt, not on the rocks, and not by briers. Jesus' setting wasn't much, but he gave the best he had. Jesus doesn't expect us to give people *the* best, but he does expect us to give them *our* best. The best staff and volunteers we can enlist, the best program we can design, the best music we can lead, the best setting we can find, and the best facilities we can provide.

> *Jesus didn't have much to work with, but he was thankful for what he had.*

Fifth, Jesus' disciples were overwhelmed by the challenge of feeding 5,000 hungry campers with no kitchen, no refrigerators, no sinks, no serving utensils, and no food! Before he addressed the problem, Jesus divided the people into groups of between 50 and 100 people each. These smaller clusters presented challenges that were 1% to 2% of the overwhelming problem. The *Principle of Chewable Bites* says that we need to break big challenges into manageable parts. A large financial challenge is broken into bite-size pieces by a budget. The extended challenge of a week's worth of activities is divided into a meaningful schedule. And the eager and willing band of staff and volunteers is structured and synchronized through job descriptions and organizational charts.

Sixth, Jesus didn't have much to work with, but he was thankful for what he had. He demonstrated the *Principle of Gratitude*. He did not grouse about the few ingredients available to him or complain that he was under supplied. He simply used what he had and was thankful for a little boy's generous heart and the meager food supply. Ultimately, he turned his grateful eyes toward his loving and powerful heavenly Father and gave thanks for God's provision.

Seventh, there is no one-best-way of doing camp ministry. Jesus taught the massive crowd, organized small groups, and healed and challenged individuals. The *Principle of Strategic Engagement* directs us to match our style of ministry with our desired outcomes and the needs of the campers. Jesus did not fall in love with only one style of ministry, nor did he apply only one method. He adapted his ministry style to strategically engage and influence his campers in the best ways possible.

Eighth, at the conclusion of the miracle, after everyone was full and satisfied, Jesus demonstrated the *Principle of Stewardship*. He said, *Let nothing be wasted*. Good stewardship is a responsibility everyone should shoulder, but especially those in the Christian camping arena—where God's creation is our chapel. But stewardship goes well beyond the physical world. Wise Christian camping leaders must strategically use every meal, every game, every song, every squabble, every mistake, every victory, and every disappointment as teaching moments to ensure that we *let nothing be wasted*.

Ninth, while Jesus was feeing 5,000 *campers*, he was also strategically engaging his *staff members*. He was modeling the *Principle of Dual Impact*. The needs of the 5,000 were different from those of the Twelve, and Jesus maintained a deeper relationship with the Twelve than he did with the 5,000. Each group had its own unique challenges, and both needed Jesus' input and direction. Camp is for the campers, but it is also for the staff members. Camp leaders need to design authentic yet different ministry strategies for the spiritual growth and welfare of *both* staff members and campers.

Tenth, at the conclusion of this amazing miracle, no one mistook Jesus for a priest, but they did think he was a prophet (possibly *The Prophet* anticipated to precede the coming of the Messiah). No one confused him with the leader of a local synagogue, but they did see him as one who had a special role to play in the spiritual development of Israel. He lived the *Principle of the Big Body*. Some camp ministries are the extension of a local church, but many camps are run by those working outside a local church structure. Priests and prophets of the Old Testament had distinct yet complementary roles, and so do the leaders of local church and (for lack of a better word) para-church ministries.

The discussion and application questions at the end of each chapter are provided to facilitate personal reflection and professional dialogue. Volunteers, staff members, summer staff, and board members can interact with these principles. They can be applied in churches, schools, missionary agencies, and any ministry organization that desires to serve God and follow Jesus' pattern of ministry engagement.

Christian camping is found around the globe. Different parts of the world express this amazing ministry in a variety of unique and culturally contextualized ways. But all of us can learn and improve as we study the principles of ministry modeled by Christian camping's all-time greatest camp director, Jesus! My prayer is that God will use these ten principles to enable camps, churches, and other ministries to operate more effectively as we follow the patterns that Jesus, the Master of Ministry, has provided.

CHAPTER ONE
THE PRINCIPLE OF INTENTIONALITY

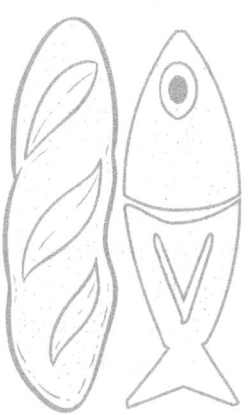

So many needs – so little time! Ministry opportunities constantly come our way. Legitimate physical and spiritual needs persistently call for our time and attention, whether or not we have the ministry bandwidth to address them. We cannot control when needy people enter our lives or pick and choose which hurting people we encounter. They just show up. Setting boundaries and establishing limits are fine, but the realities of life do not always fit our plans. We must be intentional as we direct our passions and interests and use our limited resources wisely to make the greatest impact possible.

I try to follow the old adage, *plan your work and work your plan*. But life rarely flows that way for me, and it seemingly didn't work that way for Jesus and his disciples. While their plans led them toward a few days of rest and relaxation with Jesus, life's events changed significantly creating an about-face and a radically new plan.

Jesus and the Twelve were grieving the murderous death of John the Baptist. He was Jesus' second cousin, he baptized Jesus, and he was the first mentor for several of the Lord's disciples. The Twelve had also just returned from a short-term mission trip where they proclaimed God's

Kingdom, saw lives transformed, and witnessed God's power overwhelm the evil spirits of darkness.

Physically, emotionally, and spiritually, the disciples were spent. They needed a break. They were ready to kick-back, relax, and process what they had just experienced – a staff retreat to sort through their experiences was the ideal plan. So, they packed lightly and headed out for a refreshing adventure across the Sea of Galilee.

As camping leaders know, true adventure always involves an uncertain outcome. And for the disciples, their expected outcome was about to unravel, and a new adventure emerge.

Matthew records the start of their adventure this way: *When Jesus heard what had happened* (the death of John the Baptist), *he withdrew by boat privately to a solitary place* (Matthew 14:13). These plans did not last long. *Hearing of this, the crowds followed him on foot from the towns. When Jesus landed and saw a large crowd, he had compassion on them and healed their sick* (Matthew 14:14).

Even though their *plans* didn't last long, Jesus' *purpose* and *priorities* did. More important than our plans are our *purpose* and our *priorities*. Purpose describes *why* we do *what* we do. Planning determines *what* we do and the sequence we follow. Priorities determine which things we do and do not do. Jesus put the needs of hurting people above his personal desire for refreshment and above the desires of his tired interns. He knew the needs of the Twelve aligned with his purpose for entering this world and the *priorities* under which he operated.

Planning is critical if we are to be effective in ministry. But planning requires a clear *purpose* and a commitment to well established dynamic *priorities*. Without meaningful priorities and an operational purpose, planning becomes little more than the selection and sequencing of the most attractive options. Like Jesus, we need to begin with our purpose, then design our plans, and along the way make strategic adjustments based upon our dynamic priorities.

Purpose

Jesus' well-established purpose overcame his need to relax. His deeply held commitments determined the response he and the disciples had to the crowd that followed them. An intentional response to the needs around us requires a deep commitment to a well-defined purpose, as well as a willingness to adjust based upon our predetermined priorities.

> *So long staff retreat, hello ministry!*

The huge crowd that met them included *many* people in physical distress – but *all* needed spiritual instruction. Jesus never compromised his ministry purpose, but he did jettison his intended retreat. Despite being drained and distracted, Jesus and his band of disciples reverted to the bigger purpose of seeking and saving the lost (Luke 19:10). Their purpose placed the needs of others ahead of their own comfort. They chose not to be served but to serve others (Mark 10:45).

So long staff retreat, hello ministry!

Remaining true to his purpose, Jesus met the needs of the crowd in three ways: he taught them what they needed to know, healed those in misery, and proclaimed the Kingdom of God.

Knowing the purpose for camp and answering the question *why* helps us know how to use our time, money, staff, and equipment wisely. Jesus described his purpose several times, but these four passages summarize the core of why he came.

- Matthew recalls Jesus saying, *"I have not come to call the righteous, but sinners"* (Matthew 9:13b).
- Mark records, *"For even the Son of Man did not come to be served, but to serve, and to give his life as a ransom for many"* (Mark 10:45).
- Luke states, *"For the Son of Man came to seek and to save what was lost"* (Luke 19:10).
- John tells us, *"I have come that they may have life, and have it to the full"* (John 10:10b).

Each gospel writer affirms a different aspect of Jesus' intentional mission. He came to proclaim the good news, help others, and see lives transformed. He stayed true to his purpose of seeking, serving, and saving others.

Planning

Once our purpose is clear, effective planning can begin. Just because plans change does not mean planning is unimportant—quite the opposite. Planning is critical. Well-run camps require detailed preparation. To achieve the greatest impact possible, thoughtful plans must be established. Planning helps maximize the impact of our limited time at camp and creates the context for life-changing, and eternity-altering decisions.

> *There are times when he wants to teach us not to worship our planning and preparation more than him.*

Planning is good stewardship. It enables us to focus our limited resources, direct our efforts, and effectively utilize our time, money, and people. Planning provides opportunity for us to make the biggest impact possible as we attempt to accomplish what God has called us to do. This is discussed further in Chapter 5 - *The Principle of Chewable Bites*.

Normally, the Holy Spirit leads during prayerful planning. That seems to be God's standard methodology. In general, God honors detailed preparation and planning with positive outcomes. But he is big enough, wise enough, and creative enough to change our plans as he sees fit. There are times when he wants to teach us not to worship our planning and preparation more than him.

Planning, as any good sailor knows, involves two things: 1) understanding the condition of the ship, and 2) knowing the weather forecast. The camp *ship* has eight significant areas to assess.

- Governance – Is the board, or governing body, engaged, wise, unified, concerned, aware, and conscientious?
- Staff – Are staff members skilled, experienced, committed, trained, supervised, and evaluated?
- Programs – Are the programs innovative, effective, fun, safe, attractive, and meaningful?
- Finances – Is cash flow well-managed, income adequate, expenses controlled, donations on target, and reports timely and accurate?
- Facilities – Are buildings and machinery well-maintained? Do roofs leak, are the grounds well cared for, is there equilibrium between the number of beds, dining space, meeting space, and recreational options?
- Systems – Are internal operating systems working well to support the ministry: food service, housekeeping, maintenance, registration, and development?
- Public Relations – Are people within the camp's sphere of influence aware of the good things under-

way? Do they know how they can participate, and how they can help?
- Technology – Is the website accurate and attractive? Is the online registration process streamlined? Is the internal communication fluid? And are helpful reports generated rapidly?

Planning begins with an honest, objective look *inside,* at the condition of the ship. Next, good sailors look *outside* and check the weather report. Camping leaders can influence what takes place inside their ship, but what happens outside is beyond their control. They need to address each set of realities differently.

Looking at the weather report, planners must ask, *is there clear sailing ahead, or are there storm clouds on the horizon.* What economic, cultural, political, or religious changes are underway that will impact the camp and the people being served? What is the likelihood that these changes will significantly impact the ministry? How disruptive might each of these changes be to the status quo? How might these changes be addressed to create greater ministry opportunities? Essentially, external ministry planning first asks, what is the likelihood of a trend continuing or increasing? And second, how significant or serious an impact might each trend have on the camp?

Planning not only involves assessing the realities inside and outside of the camp, it also requires the challenging work of selecting and sequencing the best available options to achieve the well-articulated purpose. After the heavy lifting of articulating the purpose is finished and the planning process complete, the hard work of implementing the plan begins. As management guru Peter Drucker once said, *All planning must deteriorate into work*!

Since few things work exactly the way they are designed, we need to be ready to adjust the plan. Dynamic priorities become critical when we face the challenges of adapting our work to fit the realities of camp life.

Priorities

All too often circumstances change, altering our plans. We cannot anticipate every potentiality that may come our way. At times we are forced to adapt new methods of ministry and demonstrate versatility as situations evolve. The meal is late, the speaker goes long, rain-rain-more rain, the pool turns green, a camper learns her grandfather has died, the horses get out of the pasture, sickness, accidents, on and on with seemingly out-of-control variables.

So, how do we respond – in anger because our plans no longer fit the realities of camp? With an exasperated, *What now Lord*? Or with honest desperation as Peter prayed as he was sinking into the waves on the Sea of Galilee, *Lord, save me*!

When our plans are disrupted by failure, crisis, or new ministry opportunities, our priorities should take control. *Priorities* should be consistent with our *purpose* and woven into the fabric of our *plans*. Jesus responded to his 5,000 unexpected campers by seamlessly changing from staff-retreat mode to teaching and healing mode, and he did it by applying his priorities. He could modify his plans and adapt to the changing situation because he was already on task to fulfill his objective in the best way possible.

Throughout any effective planning process, priorities should be established, articulated, and reviewed. Priorities help define which activities are truly important. They help us remember *what* we are trying to accomplish, as well as our commitment to *how* we will behave along the way. For some people, peace and prosperity are the dual drivers of life. For others beauty, power, fame, or recognition may be at the motivational center of their lives. For Jesus, helping others and training his disciples seemed to be his primary priorities.

> *With God at the center, we structure our lives so that God impacts and influences every other priority we engage.*

Limited time, money, and energy are the factors that force us to define our priorities. If we had unlimited resources, we could do everything we wanted. However, God has designed us with limited resources, so, we must make tough choices. To get where we hope to go, we must say 'no' to good options – sometimes very good options like staff retreats – so that we can say 'yes' to things that are better aligned with God's big purpose.

There are two ways to approach priorities: hierarchically or dynamically. On the surface the hierarchical approach seems simple and powerful, **Jesus** first, **Others** second, and **You** third is the formula for **JOY!** But what does it mean to put Jesus first? What does it mean to put others second? What does it mean to put yourself third? And is there a fourth? What if I am required to work on Sundays? Have I allowed God to slip out of first place when I miss church? And what about a business trip? If I leave my family for a week of meetings, have I shuffled the list and demolished my opportunity for Joy? What if I'm sick? Am I still required to care for others before myself or am I at liberty to spend time healing and recovering?

Hierarchical priorities are fine, but there are many situations where the list seems inadequate and more guilt producing than beneficial. A more helpful approach is the dynamic system. The *dynamic* method of determining priorities has three elements, 1) recognizing our limits, 2) placing God at the center of our lives, and 3) deciding what we will allow into our lives and what we will reject. Let's look at all three of these elements.

Recognizing our limits. Too often we make the subtle, yet fatal assumption that we are God. Christian camping leaders can be especially susceptible to this insidious temptation. We don't say it out loud, and would never admit it publicly, but in practice, we assume omnipotence. We think we can do more and more and take on every project and opportunity that comes our way. Our fear of missing out, our desire to be loved, or our need to be needed, all drive us to say *'yes'* to more than we can accomplish or handle well. We assume that we possess the God-like quality of limitless capacity. Our challenge is to use well the gifts entrusted to us, and trust God with the results.

Placing God at the center of our lives. Instead of starting with God at the top of a list, let's start with God at the center of a circle. With God at the center, we structure our lives so that God impacts and influences every other priority we engage. But we must first settle the issue of his centrality, and there can only be one thing at the center of our lives. Are we striving to build everything in our lives around all that we know and love about God? Or are we asking him to bless our own plans, and desires for whatever we determine to be a successful life? Once God is central in our lives, we build from the center, adding whatever we can fit into the rest of the circle.

Selecting Priorities. With God at the center of our lives, and with a recognition that we can only do so much, we ask, which options should I select and emphasize to best fulfill my purpose in life. The old adage, *first things first and second things not at all,* might be modified to say, *God central, second things inside our lives and everything else out.*

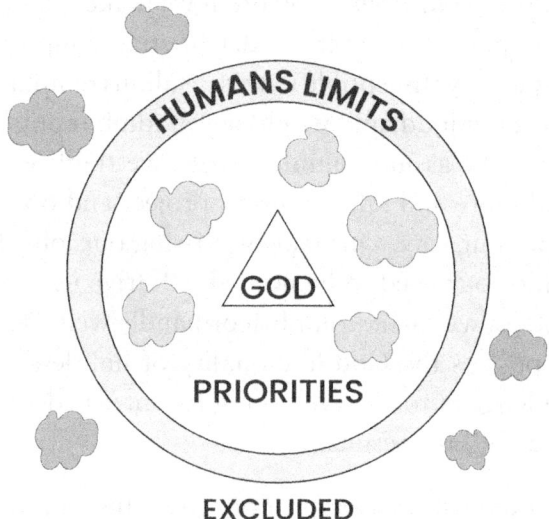

Let's start with the idea of *second things.* For me, family is not second, work third, church fourth, sleep fifth, eating sixth, and fishing seventh! In my world, each of those important components of my life plays an essential part. When God is at the center of our lives, we gather a dynamic and sacred collection of *seconds,* family, work, church, sleeping, eating, and even fishing all tie for second place.

These *seconds* are dynamic because the significance I give them ebbs and flows depending upon the circumstances. If I have a major project due at work, there is a high likelihood that I will limit my sleep time, not go fishing, and I might spend less time with my family. And that will suffice in the short run. Because next week I might take time-off from work to attend a child's play, enjoy a leisurely lunch with my wife, or go fishing. Life is not so predictable that we can allocate the same amount of time, energy, and resources to each area of our lives every day, week, month, or year. Our lives are seldom routine; rather they are filled with an ever-changing flow of crises, routines, and opportunities. Seasons come and go. Life looks different in a house full of cribs and diapers than it does with volleyballs and homework assignments. And it looks much different when the kids are in college, married, or dropping off the grandkids for the weekend! We must be willing to adjust as circumstances dictate and always strive to honor our priorities.

Jesus did just that. He knew his life's purpose, made his plans, and set his priorities. Then he adjusted his life in response to the fluid circumstances around him. Like Christ, camp directors must know their purpose, craft their plans, and modify their activities using dynamic priorities as circumstances evolve.

Jesus knew the situational changes before they arose. And as the master teacher he prepared his disciples by modeling the versatility they would need as they went into all the world to preach the gospel. And we, too, should learn and live the *Principle of Intentionality*.

Discussion Questions

1. What question should start all planning sessions? Why is this so important?

2. What is your camp's mission/purpose statement? How can your decision-making, planning, and camp activities become more closely aligned to this mission / purpose statement?

3. What are some reasons that ministry at camp can be very busy and draining? How might setting institutional, dynamic priorities help simplify your camp's ministry?

Personal Reflections

1. Do you have a personal mission/purpose statement? If not, write a first draft and commit to reviewing and rewriting it periodically.

2. What life limits do you find difficult to accept? Why do you think this is true?

3. What dynamic priorities should you embrace? What things in your life should you abandon?

CHAPTER TWO
THE PRINCIPLE OF HOLISTIC ENGAGEMENT

The camp I attended as a boy had a huge tabernacle. The rectangular building had a big stage, a dirt floor, wooden panels along each side that could be lifted for ventilation and a giant bell in the steeple. This massive structure was the site for Bible studies, missionary stories, and lots of grand singing. On rainy days it served as a gymnasium. One strict rule was to never ring the bell. Back in those days, communication was very limited. If the bell sounded, the nearby town knew there was a fire or other emergency at camp and the volunteers would race our way.

That building provided for the spiritual and recreational needs of us campers, and it furnished protection in times of emergencies. Maybe your camp uses a gymnasium for bible teaching, worship, and sharing, as well as recreation. And it probably has a first-aid kit at the ready.

Camps provide an ideal setting to meet people's needs: physical, spiritual, and emergencies. Camps are uniquely designed places to holistically meet the complete array of human needs.

The missionary movement of the nineteenth century is often criticized for what is perceived to be its singular focus on saving people's souls from eternal damnation while neglecting the massive and excruciating physical needs of people's lives. These attacks can be muted by the many hospitals, schools, and agricultural advances that remained well after the nineteenth-century missionaries departed. No doubt, some of the criticism is warranted and we need to learn from our mistakes.

Today's emphasis on social justice, poverty relief, and creation care is also criticized. Many feel that the efforts to address injustice, mitigate human pain and suffering, and protect the planet, minimize the overt proclamation of the gospel. As many in the Church focus on the physical needs of our world, concerns arise that too much of Christianity's core is neglected or compromised. They argue that the focus on raising awareness, soliciting funds, acquiring government approval, and cooperating with non-Christian NGOs erodes the Christian distinctive.

The pendulum swings. Balance is always challenging. Neither approach is always right or wrong. Socially concerned soul-winners strive to see more done to connect humanitarian relief work with the love of Jesus Christ and the truth of his word. The challenge is to meet spiritual and physical needs in tandem—the way Jesus did!

With ease and grace, Jesus ministered to the whole person. He taught the masses with power and clarity, and he addressed a broad array of maladies that beset many of those in attendance. He ministered to both spiritual and physical needs. He was not controlled by any system that divided his activities into sacred or secular work. Rather, he compassionately and strategically met the needs of the people he encountered.

As Jesus engaged a needy throng, he gave *all* he had to meet *all* the needs of *all* the people. When Jesus saw the crowd, his initial response was emotional. Matthew records, *When Jesus landed and saw a large crowd, he had compassion on them and healed their sick* (Matthew 14:14). Mark tells us, *When Jesus landed and saw a large crowd, he had **compassion** on them, because they were like sheep without a shepherd* (Mark 6:34). He did not minimize his emotions, neither did he react thoughtlessly. With compassion Jesus responded to all the needs he encountered. His emotions, filtered through his intellect, motivated his will. Spurred on by compassion, using the power within him as the Son of God, he marshalled his resources and went to work.

> *At the core of Jesus' being he was deeply moved with sympathy for the people's needs---physical and spiritual.*

He quickly transitioned from *staff retreat coordinator* to powerful *preacher* and sensitive *servant*. Jesus used *all* of himself and everything available to him, to meet *all* the needs of *all* the people who joined him on that lonely hillside. He understood that everyone needed food, some needed healing, and each one needed the truth that he taught and embodied. Jesus provided everything the people truly needed.

His compassionate heart understood and engaged the needs of others and enabled him to focus on feeding, healing, and teaching rather than satisfying his own needs. He felt their pain—and did something about it. His emotional response was from the heart. He was moved to help. The Greek word translated *compassion* is s*planchnizomai*. The English word *spleen* finds its root in this same Greek expression. The concept means *deep within*. At the core of Jesus' being he was deeply moved with sympathy for the people's needs—physical and spiritual. They needed help, he felt their pain, and he did something about it.

Both Matthew and Mark focus on Jesus' *compassion*, but they emphasize two very different responses flowing from his heart of deep compassion. Matthews says, *he had compassion on them and healed their sick* (Matthew 14:14). Mark says, *he had compassion on them . . . So he began to teach them many things* (Mark 6:34). Luke does not mention Jesus' emotional reaction but notes his attention to both spiritual and physical needs. Luke says, *he welcomed them and spoke to them about the Kingdom of God, and healed those who needed healing* (Luke 9:11).

Jesus engaged the crowd on at least three levels. Let's view these, not necessarily in sequential order, but in three distinct spheres of attention. First, he *reached out to those with painful, immediate needs:* those who were blind, lame, or diseased. The people who needed medical attention received his healing touch. Their bodies were made well and the special circumstances that dominated their lives were addressed and healed.

Second, *Jesus taught them many things.* He taught the masses deep, universal truth about the Kingdom of God, all the while teaching his disciples a laser-focused theological lesson on Christology, *who* he was and *what* he could do for them. He addressed their spiritual needs in various ways, but never at the expense of their physical needs.

> *Camp creates a unique context to minister to the whole person.*

Third, Jesus fed the multitude. Jesus relieved the intense, painful needs of those suffering from injury or disease, and he met the spiritual needs of the entire group by teaching them many things and explaining to them the Kingdom of God. But he also met their shared, ongoing, physical requirement for food when he multiplied the loaves and

THE PRINCIPLE OF HOLISTIC ENGAGEMENT

fish. The people were hungry, and Jesus knew they had set aside their regular meal schedule to come and listen to him preach. Like Mary, they had abandoned their kitchen responsibilities and had chosen what is better (Luke 10:42). And Jesus was willing to honor their decision and meet this real, albeit commonplace, need as well.

Jesus does it all. Jesus meets us at our point of pain, he knows what we need to develop spiritually, and he provides for our ongoing needs as well. Jesus seamlessly healed, taught, and fed the people. Within one encounter he addressed temporal and eternal needs and confronted physical and spiritual pain.

Our error today is generally one of emphasis. We are quick to criticize a person or group whose focus seems to be too heavenly minded to be of any earthly good, or too earthly minded to be of any heavenly good. Jesus would have none of it. He saw people as complete beings with needs that required a loving response, not problems to be ignored or opportunities to be exploited. He saw people through compassionate eyes and looked for ways to help.

Camp creates a unique context to minister to the whole person. Churches are designed for spiritual engagement with facilities and programs that enhance teaching and worship. Hospitals create a setting for God's love and mercy to be extended to those who are suffering and in crisis. Social service institutions demonstrate God's grace and care by feeding the hungry and providing shelter. But camp ministry, by engaging people over an extended time and in new places, creates a context where all three styles of ministry are demonstrated.

A camp's infirmary provides special care for the sick and injured. Nurses minister to those with special physical needs. There are also Bible teachers, small group leaders, and counselors ready to address spiritual needs. And the food service, housekeeping, and maintenance departments stand ready to serve the routine needs of all who attend. Camps provide amazing opportunities to meet campers' spiritual, physical, and emotional needs. Meeting these needs takes place in both routine and unusual circumstances.

We are complex people. The union between the material and immaterial aspects of our lives is easy to see on a superficial level, but inscrutable as we dive deeper. What we do know is that there is an interconnection between our physical and our spiritual lives. Jesus did not focus on the spiritual at the expense of the physical, nor did he neglect the spiritual to engage people's physical needs.

As a good camp director, Jesus cared graciously for the campers in crisis, taught truth to all, and abundantly met their ongoing needs. He lived the *Principle of Holistic Engagement*.

Discussion Questions

1. In what ways is your camp addressing all of your campers' needs: physical, emotional, and spiritual?

2. How can your camp be more proactive in meeting the physical needs of your campers and guests? What about meeting spiritual needs?

3. How do you think the disciples felt as they watched Jesus heal the sick and teach the multitude?

4. Do you think spiritual needs can be met while physical needs are unmet? Why or why not?

Personal Reflections

1. What ministry style utilizes your gifts and provides you with the greatest satisfaction: meeting physical needs or spiritual needs? Is your current role aligned with your gifts, and does it provide satisfaction in ministry?

2. Do you enjoy resolving dramatic, highly intense crises, like when Jesus healed hurting people? Or do you prefer more routine, low-stress interactions like when Jesus taught, organized, and fed people?

3. What physical needs or spiritual needs do you think you are most gifted to meet?

CHAPTER THREE
THE PRINCIPLE OF INABILITY

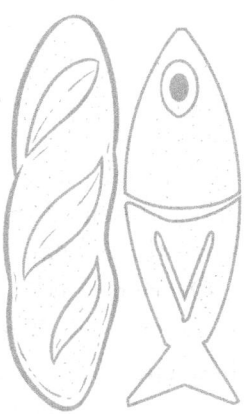

I wanted to go home, see my family, take a nap, watch a ball game, and recoup from a busy week of camp. However, a very disturbing domestic conflict within a guest family came to a head and my time off evaporated. I had no idea what to do. Calls with attorneys, ours and theirs, consultation with board members, wisdom from the family's pastors, and some impromptu prayer meetings seemed to calm the tension. I just wanted everyone to go home – so that I could too. I'm a camp director, not a family therapist!

But things went from bad to worse. A few hours later the county sheriff showed up to let me know I'd been charged with kidnapping! So long quite afternoon and evening. Why won't this problem just go away?

The sheriff understood the nature of the complaint, asked enough questions to file a report, and then told me not to worry. Easy for him to say. Two-to-ten years in one of Texas' fine 'stone hotels' is all that I could get for kidnapping.

I felt overwhelmed, hopeless, and totally inadequate to meet the challenge of that hot afternoon. However, God was at work and a few days later the family received the help they needed – at least to the point where we could run camp without major drama in the parking lot.

The disciples anticipated a relaxing time of celebration and reflection. Instead, it was back to work, and what a job it was! Their expectations were forced to make a hard 180-degree turn, and as if the whiplash was not bad enough Jesus presented them with an impossible challenge and an unworkable plan.

Overwhelmed! They could not face one more insurmountable challenge. By the end of the day the disciples had enough and begged Jesus to make the problem go away. "Send them home," they cried. "We have no food, no money, no nothing. Send them away! We are tired and need a break!" Let's look at the unanimous opinion of the four gospel accounts.

- Matthew 14:15, *Send the crowds away, so they can go to the villages and buy some food.*
- Mark 6:36, *Send the people away so that they can go to the surrounding countryside and villages and buy themselves something to eat.*
- Luke 9:12, *Send the crowd away so they can go to the surrounding villages and countryside and find food and lodging.*
- John 6:7, *It would take a half year's wages to buy enough bread for each one to have a bite!*

Jesus called His disciples to an impossible challenge. They were overwhelmed and painfully aware of their lack of resources. His command, *You give them something to eat* (Matthew 14:16, Mark 6:37, Luke 9:13) was at best nonsensical, and at worst, humiliating. What were they supposed to do, feed 5,000 people with no groceries, no kitchen, and no food service staff?

Jesus' challenge was not cruel or heartless. The test was intentional and developmental. The task was designed to demonstrate the disciples' inability and to remind them of

THE PRINCIPLE OF INABILITY

their human limitations. Jesus' call, to accomplish the impossible, should have reminded them to rely upon him for every resource they needed: physical, spiritual, organizational, and emotional. Instead, they seemed defeated, overwhelmed, and overmatched. They failed Christology 101. They needed a deeper understanding of who Jesus was and what he could do.

Jesus had not abandoned his *staff retreat* objectives. He merely restructured the context and redesigned the learning paradigm. Instead of a relaxed weekend away to process, debrief, and reflect, he engaged the disciples in a real-life exercise. His goal was not only to hear about the wonderful victories the Twelve had won, but he also deeply desired for them to understand God's availability and power in the face of impossible circumstances. Jesus wanted them to learn to rely on him when difficult situations arose. However, instead of facing the challenge and calling on Jesus for help, they simply begged him to send the crowd away! Jesus wanted them to reorder their thinking and to reset their default switch to *Rely-on-Jesus* when they faced overwhelming tasks.

Camps deal with many impossible challenges. Sometimes these are *physical* issues: bills are due, but the bank account is empty, campers are coming, but the new building is not yet ready to occupy, registration is open but the website has crashed. Sometimes the challenges are *relational* and *emotional*: the program is running late and food service is fuming, the board is split five-to-five on adopting the new strategic plan, and the injured camper's parents are threatening a lawsuit. But many of the challenges are *spiritual*: changes in the worship style have angered the guests; a camper rejects the gospel and is vocal about his disdain for camp and Christianity; gossip, bickering, and envy divide the summer staff; and a camper shares confidential details of her abuse at home.

My first response is to throw up my hands and exclaim the words Isaiah ascribes to the reluctant leaders of Israel, *I have no remedy. I have no food or clothing in my house; do not make me the leader of the people* (Isaiah 3:7). Like the prophets of old, we too, often ask, why me Lord? We have enough problems of our own and feel totally inadequate to resolve the traumas and dramas of camp.

> *He wanted them to know, beyond a shadow of a doubt, that he is sufficient to match any challenge that would come their way. And he wants us to know that as well.*

If we can step back and reflect objectively, that is not a bad place to be! The critical issue is not feeling inadequate, but it is how we respond. What do we do next? Jesus wanted the disciples to feel their overwhelming inadequacy and look to him to solve their problem. He wanted them to experience the limits of their humanity and turn to him for help.

They failed the test!

The disciples tried three solutions, the very ones we still try today. First, they thought about money. Philip responded, *even if we had an emergency fundraising appeal and scraped together eight months wages, we still could not solve the problem* (my paraphrase of John 6:7).

Andrew demonstrated the second tactic we often use, gathering all available resources. He located a boy with a lunch and a generous heart. But those morsels would not even serve the disciples (John 6:9).

Like me, and probably you, the disciples tried a third strategy. They just wanted the problem to go away. No amount of money, materials, or hiding would match the power that was available to them, yet they seemed oblivious to their divine resources and wanted the problem to evaporate. Jesus wanted them to learn a critical lesson. He wanted them to know, beyond a shadow of a doubt, that he is sufficient to match any challenge that would come their way. And he wants us to know that as well.

There are two complimentary truths at play in this story. *First*, Jesus wants his disciples to learn their inadequacy and to see that they will face massive challenges much bigger than their wisdom, strength, or talents can bear. And *second*, Jesus is eager for them to learn about his divine resources, and that he can provide everything they need to overcome any obstacle they may face. Jesus brings into focus the dual realities of, 1) human inadequacy, and 2) God's sufficiency. Both are important and fit snuggly together like a hand in a glove. Awareness of both these truths is critical in camp ministry – and in life.

During Jesus' final meal with his disciples, he reminded them, *apart from me you can do nothing* (John 15:5). When Jesus spoke those words, I wonder if any of the Twelve experienced a flash-back to that hillside in Galilee, the 5,000 hungry followers and their powerless meltdown. I'm sure a few recalled that late afternoon and their extreme frustration until Jesus reminded them of who he was.

Couple that thought with Paul's encouragement in Philippians 4:13, *I can do everything through him who gives me strength.* Again, when Peter and the other disciples read those words, I imagine that some of them relived many of Jesus' miraculous adventures. There were storms quieted, a stroll on the waves, blind eyes healed, lame legs walking, and grieving family members welcoming their loved ones back from the dead. I'd be surprised if they didn't recall participating in the impossible feeding of the massive throng with a few pieces of bread and a couple of fish.

The tasks at camp seem overwhelming at times. Some days, frustration is our constant companion. The obstacles appear insurmountable, the tensions too vast to resolve, and the needs too great to address. We need money for payroll. We are short eight summer staff. The well is running dry. The food truck is late. The program staff and food service department are at war again! The website is inaccurate. The health department is coming back for a recheck. And on and on and on!

When you reach the point of saying, *I can't do this*, Jesus is ready and willing to help. Give him what little you have and watch him multiply it for his honor and glory! He is the One to call when we reach the end of our resources and realize the truth of the *Principle of Inability*.

THE PRINCIPLE OF INABILITY

# Discussion Questions

1. Is your camp facing any overwhelming challenges? What are they?

2. What are some benefits or positive outcomes that might derive from the major challenges currently facing your camp?

3. Is there a time you can recall when God provided for your ministry, despite your camp's inability?

4. How much money would it take to fix all your camp's challenges? Would that really be enough?

Personal Reflections

1. What is your first emotional response to a major life challenge – fear, anger, excitement, or other?

2. Which verse do you resonate with the most, *I can do everything through Christ who strengthens me!* (Philippians 4:13), or, *Apart from me you can do nothing.* (John 15:5)?

3. Do you find it easier to trust God when everything is working well, or when you face significant challenges?

CHAPTER FOUR
THE PRINCIPLE OF GREEN-GRASS

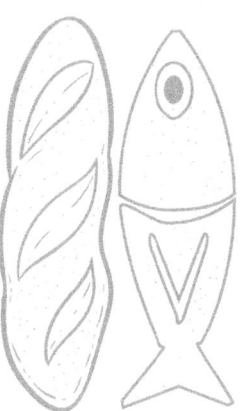

An ancient folktale describes angels distributing rocks throughout the world. Their bags break while flying over Israel, accounting for the abundance of stones covering the countryside. The exact site of the Feeding of the 5,000 is unknown, but to this day exposed rocks inundate most of the area.

Rough stones do not provide comfortable places to sit. Besides the jagged rocks, the area hosts briers and gritty soil. Listening to Jesus teach while sitting on rocks, brambles, or dirt, could have become increasingly uncomfortable for thousands of people. Every time a listener adjusted their seat the sharp rocks and briers would make themselves known, distracting the listener from the powerful and essential message Jesus was presenting.

Jesus' mountainside meeting room, overlooking the Sea of Galilee, was likely a rugged, rocky hillside punctuated with areas of green grass. The seating options were limited, but some spots were more accommodating than others. Jesus noticed the problem and addressed the peoples' need. His solution wasn't luxurious, he simply provided the best option available. John tells us, *there was plenty of grass in that place* (John 6:10). Mark records Jesus' clear instructions.

JESUS: CAMP DIRECTOR

Then Jesus directed them to have all the people sit down in groups on the green grass (Mark 6:39). So, among the dirt, rocks, briers, and weeds, Jesus instructed the people to sit down in the *green grass* – the prime seating option he had to offer.

> *Christian camps do not need to compete with five-star luxury hotels or world-class theme parks, but they should anticipate the needs of guests, meet or exceed expectations, and offer the best options possible.*

Jesus was sensitive to the needs of his *campers*. He made them as comfortable as possible. And making campers comfortable has two very desirable outcomes. *First,* comfortable surroundings *minimize distractions*. People can focus on the teaching or presentation, not squirming to find a more comfortable seating position. And *second*, providing comfortable surroundings *builds trust*. When people trust us with the little things, they are more likely to trust us with the big things, too. Let's unpack each of these and then apply the *Principle of the Green-Grass* to several areas of camp ministry.

Minimize Distractions

People are easily distracted. It doesn't take much to disrupt a train of thought and even less to derail a positive emotional experience. Avoiding unnecessary distractions is key to staying focused on the overarching mission of the camp. Any camp with a well-articulated and systemically applied mission statement will work to align all its activities to accomplish the desired results: evangelism, discipleship, team building, leadership development, or any other major emphases. To see campers' lives transformed means staying on task, and that requires avoiding, or at least minimizing, distractions.

Bad food, poor signage, cold showers, late meetings, untrained staff, inoperable websites, boring Bible studies, dirty bathrooms, untuned guitars, burned out light bulbs, or leaky sinks can distract campers physically and emotionally. Jesus didn't have much to offer his *guests,* but he gave them the best he had because he wanted to minimize distractions.

Christian camps do not need to compete with five-star luxury hotels or world-class theme parks, but they should anticipate the needs of guests, meet or exceed expectations, and offer the best options possible. Ultimately, Christian camps need to show love and hospitality to the campers and guests they serve. And they can do that by providing *green-grass* staff, *green-grass* programs, *green-grass* food service, *green-grass* administration, and *green-grass* facilities to everyone who enters their care. Doing less allows distractions to arise; these subvert the efforts of the camp and minimize its effectiveness.

Build Trust

A *green-grass* experience does much more than minimize distractions. More importantly, it helps build trust. One of the reasons camp experiences leave an indelible mark on the lives of so many campers is because of the trust that develops rapidly in the camp context. It seems rather obvious, but don't miss a simple yet powerful reality: *people trust those who demonstrate trustworthiness.* Trust flows to the trustworthy!

When wrestling with the significance of trust and striving to be trustworthy, two essential realities should be remembered. *First*, first impressions set people's default switches to "trust" or "caution." And *second*, trust is never given, it is always loaned.

Let's look at the issue of *first impressions* as it relates to camp. Today's first impression is a website. A *green-grass* website is critical to communicate both information and impressions. Is the content accurate? Do the links actually work? Are the pictures representative of the site and program? Do the dynamics draw people in and entice them to see more? Trust begins when a camper or parent says, *Wow, that was a great website!* What they subconsciously say is, *That camp does a good job with their website, I bet they will do a good job with our child's camp experience, too!*

Most people who have worked in camp very long have a story about a skeptical, hardened, teenage camper who decided long before camp started that they were going to hate every moment of their week. Upon arrival, they interpret every experience through that negative filter and the week starts miserably for everyone. But sometime during camp God worked in a powerful way. Their life was transformed, and they didn't want the week to end! Trust had grown as the trustworthiness of the staff members and the institution demonstrated God's love, grace, joy, and hope to the hardened camper.

On the other side of the coin, many years ago, long before GPS, a camper arrived for a men's weekend retreat just before midnight and he was not happy. I met him in the parking lot as I was about to head home for the night. He had been driving the rural back roads of East Texas for hours trying to find the camp, but due to poor signage and a burned-out guard-light he arrived with a couple hours of frustration and anger boiling over. We had not provided a *green-grass* arrival experience for him (and who knows how many others). Recovering from a bad start is very difficult. And in a short weekend experience, a great start is essential. Without *green-grass* there are painful distractions and the default switch is set to "caution." In the world of caution and skepticism, trust does not easily develop.

Second is the reality that *trust is never given, only loaned.* Good first impressions flip a *default switch* in people's minds to "trust," creating positive feelings that significantly influence how they interpret future interactions. Generally, people filter subsequent events through the assumptions they have already made. Even though first impressions are powerful, if future experiences contradict the initial dealings long enough, people eventually *reset* the default switch to 'caution' or 'skepticism' and withdraw their trust.

Trust can be lost through either erosion or explosion. We erode the trust of campers and guests when we do not meet their expectations, do our jobs poorly, or fail to fulfill our missional calling. Lazy, selfish, insensitive, nonchalant, or indifferent responses to needs and opportunities allow trust to drain out of a relationship. Even more important than incompetence is the impact of our character, good or bad. Trust explodes when a camp leader's character implodes. When a leader runs off with the secretary or the building fund, trust is gone in an instant.

Be intentional and honest about institutional self-examination. Ask, what could we do to serve God and our campers even better? How can we provide a more *green-grass* experience? How can we remove distractions? And what can we do to demonstrate trustworthiness? Start strong, follow-up with consistent expressions of love and care, stay true to your calling, and send campers home wishing they could stay longer.

JESUS: CAMP DIRECTOR

What does a green-grass camp look like?

We all want to give our campers and guests the best experience possible. We want them to be comfortable, free from distractions, and to develop an attitude of trust. So, what does that look like? How do we create *green-grass* camps? Camp, in its simplest form, can be divided into *People*, *Place*, and *Program*. Let's look at a *green-grass* camp from those three perspectives.

People – At its heart, camp is its staff. A great staff will overcome any shortfall in the *place* and enhance any *program*. Exceptional camps enlist wonderful staff members, people who love God, work hard, have fun, live out their commitments, and ask forgiveness when they fall short. Securing a great staff begins with recruitment, asking the best person possible to fill each position. Once in place, good people need training. They need to know what is expected, how to perform their duties, and how to respond when the wheels come off. They also need to be organized strategically, supervised caringly, and evaluated graciously. *Green-grass* staff members make all the difference.

Great staff members do not grow on trees, they must be recruited. Staff recruitment is challenging and at times frustrating. Whether paid-staff or volunteers, people have busy lives and are called in many directions. They must realize that camp is a relational ministry and that their presence and contributions are critical to the camp's success. The planning, prayer, effort, and tenacity required to secure a *green-grass* staff will be the most profitable investment a Christian camping leader can make.

Place – Camps are generally located in gorgeous places, at the base of a snow-capped mountain, along the shore of a tranquil lake, in the shade of a lush forest, or on the bank of a babbling brook. But often, the architectural design and construction techniques intrude unflatteringly into the beauty of God's creation. *Green-grass* places maximize the site and minimize the intrusion. A fresh coat of paint with a wise color palette makes everything look better. Screens repaired, gutters cleaned, erosion addressed - all support a *green-grass* experience. God called Adam to be the *Park Ranger* of the Garden of Eden, and he calls us to care for our sites as well. Comfort, related to the place, is not about opulence or extravagance. It is about providing the best we can with what we have. A backpack camp may seem minimal in terms of place. It will involve sleeping on the ground, heavy packs, blisters, and unremarkable food. But it also provides magnificent sights, memorable experiences, and meaningful solitude. A *green-grass* place, using whatever is available to work with, can make all the difference.

> *The planning, prayer, effort, and tenacity required to secure a green-grass staff will be the most profitable investment a Christian camping leader can make.*

Program – What happens at camp is critical to its success. Poor planning, disorganization, and purposeless activity can minimize the effectiveness of what campers experience, creating distractions and limiting the development of trust. *Green-grass* programming means knowing the camp's purpose and intentionally building the activities to support that purpose. Too many camps begin their program design by considering available activity alternatives. They ask, *what can we do this summer?* Instead, they should ask, *what should we do this summer?*

Addressing a few basic questions may be beneficial.

- What is the camp's purpose? Is it primarily oriented toward evangelism, discipleship, leadership development, or some other desired outcome?
- Do activities centered around competition or cooperation help fulfill your camp's purpose?
- Is there a need for high energy, large group presentations, or small group, reflective discussions?
- What type of meal service will support the camp's desired outcomes? Should you use round tables, assigned seating, and a flexible schedule after meals to encourage and extend discussion? Or would it be better to employ a cafeteria style, come-and-go approach so that campers meet new people? Is mealtime a strategic part of the program or simply an opportunity to recharge and prepare for the next activity?
- What are the characteristics and needs of each camper age-group?
- Should the schedule be packed with activity, filling every minute to keep campers busy, or should the schedule provide ample time for reflection, conversations, and responses?

There are no right or wrong answers, but there are wise, strategic, and effective methods. Provide a *green-grass* program and watch God work in campers' hearts.

How do we create a green-grass ministry?

Striving to create a *green-grass* camp experience is both simple and complex. In some ways it is like following the Golden Rule. It is not that hard – until you try to apply it to a difficult situation. There are some parallels between creating a *green-grass* experience and following the golden rule. A program built around *do unto others as you would have them do unto you* is a great place to start.

In many ways, people are pretty much the same. We all want our children to be influenced by godly, fun, committed, hard-working young people; the parents of campers do, too. We like good food; so do campers. We like to have fun and relax, but also stretch ourselves and overcome challenges; so do campers. We are not much different from those who come through the camp gate. *Do unto others as you would have them do unto you!* (Luke 6:31)

Who is your customer? And what do they value?

Even though campers and guests share many of our values and commitments, they can be very different from us in many ways. The first time I conducted an anonymous survey of family campers I included a question about household income. I provided eight options starting low and ending with a number so high I could only dream about earning that much money. When we tabulated the results, all but two of the hundred or so respondents were in the top income category! Working at camp, I didn't realize I was living with very different economic realities than our guests. The people we served lived in neighborhoods and worked in settings way beyond my experience. If we want to provide *green-grass* camp experiences, we need to study our guests, know who they are, and learn all we can about their lives, their challenges, their values, desires, and their commitments.

Long before Peter Drucker crystallized his famous marketing questions, his friend, Bob Buford was pummeling me with: *Who is your customer? And what do they value?* Bob served on the board of the first ministry I led. His probing, encouraging, and focused questions forced me to wrestle deeply with how to create a *green-grass* experience for campers and guests. His insights changed the way I think forever. Those two questions are at the heart of any *green-grass* camp. Ask them incessantly and don't settle for the first answer that comes to mind.

Jesus, the Master Camp Director, took 5,000 campers and almost nothing else, and held a powerful and effective camp. He gave them the best he had. What he had wasn't much, but he reduced distractions, built trust, and changed the lives of countless campers. He masterfully applied the *Principle of Green-Grass*.

 **Discussion Questions**

1. What aspects of your camp provide the best *green-grass* experiences for your campers? Which ones need more work?

2. What can you do, without spending any money, to make your campers' experience at your site more comfortable and beneficial?

3. What are some ways you can build greater trust at camp?

Personal Reflections

1. What do you enjoy doing at camp that provides a *green-grass* experience for your campers and guests?

2. Do you consider yourself a trustworthy person? Why or why not?

3. What are some things you can do to make yourself more worthy of others' trust?

4. Think of a person you trust. What qualities in their life make them worthy of your trust? Are those qualities evident in your life as well?

CHAPTER FIVE
THE PRINCIPLE OF CHEWABLE BITES

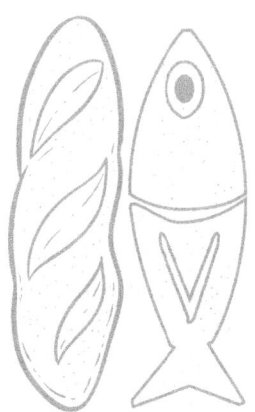

One of the oldest maxims of Christian camp is, *they will forgive you for bad theology, but never for bad food!* People take their food seriously. They like to eat, and they need to eat, especially after a long hike into the countryside and a day-long seminar. Jesus provided his 5,000 unexpected campers with excellent *theology*, but now it was dinner time.

5,000 hungry people had listened to Jesus all day. They were tired, famished, and ready to eat. But there was no food in sight. No restaurants, no food trucks, no grocery stores or vending machines—nothing. They did not appear 'hangry' or upset, just in need of nourishment. Jesus and the disciples faced a daunting challenge—how to feed 5,000 unexpected campers—any food service manager's worst nightmare.

Jesus didn't begin to solve the problem by serving food, he started by organizing the hungry people. He didn't begin divvying the *loaves and the fish*, he began divvying the *crowd*. Any big challenge requires organizational management, and Jesus was a master of organization. He didn't over-engineer his response, nor did he allow chaos to reign.

JESUS: CAMP DIRECTOR

Let's look at how Jesus responded to the huge challenge before him.

The disciples were overwhelmed as they surveyed the 5,000 hungry people covering the Galilean hillside. Their response (as we saw in Chapter 3) was unanimous, *send the crowds away*. The problem was massive, and the disciples felt totally inadequate to meet the challenge. The task was huge, and they were incapable of responding to the enormous problem confronting them. Their solution – *send them away*! And that is the way we often respond when problems look too big, we just want them to go away.

All camps must address three basic challenges that deserve high quality management attention: money, time, and people.

Jesus, however, had a better idea. He saw the problem not an *insurmountable obstacle*, but as an *immense opportunity*. This opportunity needed structure, so he divided the crowd into groups of 50 or 100 (Mark 6:40). This strategic, organizational decision benefited the disciples more than anyone. The math is straight forward, 50 is 1% of 5,000 and 100 is 2%. Jesus divided the huge crowd (and huge challenge) into 1% and 2% tasks. By fracturing the problem into smaller pieces, he hoped to move his disciples away from their sense of discouragement and defeat to a more hopeful place. His strategy involved organizing the problem into smaller, more manageable pieces. The overwhelming problem was now a collection of much smaller, less threatening tasks. These were, as my mother used to say, *chewable bites!*

Follow my math – if the average size group was 75 people, there would have been about 65-70 groups. Divided between the Twelve Disciples, each would be responsible for serving five or six groups. Using this organizational tactic, Jesus gave each disciple a more significant, yet manageable number of small groups. The problem was still daunting, but now there was some structure and organization to what had been one, gigantic impossibility.

A little organizational framework did not diminish the immensity of the miracle. Jesus' supernatural power was not minimized by the management structure. He simply broke a huge problem into many smaller pieces so that his disciples could gain confidence as they approached the enormous challenge in 1% or 2% segments.

Whatever the task, good management breaks work into achievable, bite-sized pieces and assigns these tasks to qualified workers. Program leaders, counselors, nurses, lifeguards, worship leaders, Bible teachers, food service staff, maintenance workers, all do their parts. Camps need organizational structure to accomplish what God has put before them.

Camping leaders face three fundamental responsibilities that can appear insurmountable. All camps must address three basic challenges that deserve high quality management attention: *money, time,* and *people*. Money challenges are divided by budgets, time is arranged by schedules, and people coordinated through job descriptions and organizational charts. Each of these management tools, *budgets, schedules,* and *job descriptions and organizational charts*, divide big challenges into manageable parts. Let's look at each of these three and examine their *chewable bites*.

Money

Not many people get into Christian camping because they love budgets, financial statements, and fundraising campaigns. However, dealing with money comes with the territory. If you want to be a camp director, then you need to manage money. In doing so, there are always five variables that camp directors, and their leadership teams, need to address:

- Price: *How much should we charge?*
- Volume: *How many campers will attend?*
- Quality: *What level of service will we provide?*
- Cost: *Is this the best price we can find? (And do we really need this?)*
- Subsidy: *How much money do we need to raise?*

For our purposes, let's look at just the fundraising issue as a model of how to apply the *Principle of Chewable Bites* to a daunting financial challenge. Imagine a camp that needs to raise $1,000,000 for a capital campaign and its current contribution income is about $50,000 a year. Without addressing the validity of the project or the credibility of the organization (and its representatives), finding $1,000,000 may appear to be an insurmountable challenge, until applying the *Principle of Chewable Bites*.

Just like Jesus, begin by dividing the challenge into 1% and 2% segments, $10,000 and $20,000 parts. Those amounts are still significant, but much less threatening than the entire campaign. Jesus had 12 *interns*; possibly the camp could enlist 12 volunteers to help take on some of the work. A volunteer team might include some to approach churches while others host special events in major cities. Another group might contact former campers and summer staff members. Some may be willing to write foundation grants. A few others might make personal calls meeting one on one with potential major donors.

THE PRINCIPLE OF CHEWABLE BITES

When broken into smaller bites, the $1,000,000 challenge could look like this:

Audience/Project	Number of Responses	Amount over three years	Total
Churches	20	$10,000	$200,000
Special Events	5	$20,000	$100,000
Former Staff	50	$1,000	$50,000
Foundations	2	$100,000	$200,000
Major Donors	5	$50,000	$250,000
Other Donors	40	$5,000	$200,000
TOTAL	122		$1,000,000

Campaigns rarely play out the way they are designed. However, when we face a huge challenge instead of many smaller challenges, we, like the disciples, may only wring our hands and hope the challenge just goes away. Fundraising is never easy. It takes effort, tenacity, and the ability to overcome adversity. However, as a massive endeavor is divided into *chewable bites*, hope can be restored.

Time

A week of camp or a weekend retreat consists of many short segments. Like a 500-piece jigsaw puzzle, the entire event is comprised of hundreds of tiny, discrete, yet interlocking, events. Like the puzzle, each of these camp pieces is interconnected with its surrounding events. What happens before breakfast influences breakfast. What takes place in the morning impacts lunch, lunchtime flows into the afternoon and so forth throughout the day.

Assuming that a well-articulated purpose statement sets the backdrop for all planning decisions, the critical question is, how will each segment within the day help accomplish the camp's purpose? Continuing the puzzle illustration, how will each piece add to the magnificent life-changing picture that God is developing throughout the total camp experience?

When considering camp scheduling, three words are critical: *sequence, transition,* and *flexibility*. Schedules should disaggregate the week, or weekend, into many individual yet related parts. *Sequence* will explain the order of events. *Transition* describes the connection between events. *Flexibility* recognizes that things rarely go exactly as planned.

Sequence simply acknowledges that information, relationships, and trust are built one step at a time. What do campers need to learn in horseback riding today, to ensure that tomorrow will be safe, fun, and educational? What do canoers need to demonstrate on flat water before they enter rapids? What safety procedures do campers need to learn on the ground before engaging a ropes course 24-feet in the air. The many smaller pieces of camp must be assembled into a logical and strategic sequence. When do reluctant campers let down their guard and fully participate in the camp activities? How long does it take to build adequate trust to address crucial issues? At what point in the week do campers begin to measure time based upon the end of camp rather than the beginning? All those issues, and more, should be contemplated as the small segments of camp-time are designed and sequenced.

Transitions modulate the dynamics of a camp experience. Swells of enthusiasm give way to quiet moments of contemplation. Active games flow into periods of rest and recuperation. Large group meetings disaggregate into small group discussions and eventually into one-on-one conversations. Seamlessly transitioning between the many discrete moments of camp creates a secure and comfortable environment. Migrating campers emotionally from where they are to where you want them to be requires sensitivity, skill, planning, and wisdom. Great camp directors take fun very seriously!

Flexibility does not assume a hasty, last-minute decision. Flexibility requires that alternative plans have been prepared in case rain, sickness, burnt lasagna, or long-winded speakers, doom the original design. A jump-rope nearby, a handy guitar for spontaneous singing, brain teasers, memory verse reviews, relay races, or conversation starting questions can all be at the ready in case circumstances demand modifications to our well-designed plan.

People

While teaching a group of Christian camping leaders in Kenya, I asked the question, *How do you eat an elephant?* I expected the group to respond, *One bite at a time!* Instead, I saw blank stares and quizzical looks.

After the seminar, a young man asked me, *Why would anyone try to eat an elephant by themself? If you want to eat an elephant, you call the whole village!*

My Western, individualistic approach told me to divide the task into bite-sized pieces, but to do the work myself. My African friend had a better idea, divide the work, and allow others to help accomplish the gigantic challenge.

There are two ways for a group to approach any task: as a well-designed team or as a mob! A job description explains what is expected of each staff member and an organizational chart connects the group into an effective and

JESUS: CAMP DIRECTOR

efficient team. Whether paid staff or volunteers, the prospect of recruiting, hiring, training, organizing, supervising, and evaluating staff can seem ominous. Whether recruiting volunteers or hiring staff, finding good, godly, committed, skilled people is a difficult but critical task.

Imagine a youth pastor who is responsible to organize a weekend retreat that will occur in four months. About 100 junior high school students are expected and an estimated 30-35 volunteer staff members will be needed. How to start? Where does one look for so many competent staff members? Who should do what? How does one fill all these positions with the right volunteers? By applying the *Principle of Chewable Bites*.

The leader or leadership team needs to identify the key roles that need to be fulfilled and then find the best people possible to fill them. That overwhelming challenge requires some time-bound *chewable bites*.

Classification or Title	Number Needed	By January	By February	By March
Program Director	1	1		
Program Helpers	2			2
Worship Leader	1	1		
Worship Band	3		3	
Boys' Counselors	10	4	3	3
Girls' Counselors	10	4	3	3
Nurse	1		1	
Lifeguards	2		2	
Total	30	10	12	8

Finding the right staff is just part of the process. They also need to be trained, supervised, and evaluated. But each of these daunting tasks can be structured in a way to provide hope that the work will be accomplished in the time allowed. Organizing the work into smaller more manageable parts provides a sense of control. Once planned, discipline is required to stay on schedule. And again, plans rarely work the way the are designed. However, having a plan with *chewable bites* helps the leader sleep at night.

Most people are overwhelmed by big challenges and monstrous problems. But those big, frightening, crushing difficulties can all be restructured into a collection of 1% and 2% mini-obstacles. Once the problem is restructured, it can be faced with less fear and greater hope.

Jesus divided the vast challenge facing the disciples into 1% and 2% tasks to enable them to address the foreboding work with a renewed hope. A critical job of Christian camp leaders is to structure the never-ending and seemingly insurmountable tasks of camp into *chewable bites*. Staff members, volunteers, board members, donors, and yes, we ourselves need the hope that comes by applying the *Principle of Chewable Bites*.

Discussion Questions

1. What overwhelming challenge seems humanly impossible for your camp? What can you do to organize your work into smaller components?

2. Of the three areas of administration (money, time, and people), which one does your camp manage best? Which one needs some improvement?

3. Which members of your team are especially gifted in breaking major projects into "*Chewable Bites?*"

Personal Reflections

1. Are you facing a big personal challenge? What can you do to divide it into smaller, more manageable parts?

2. Which area of management do you find most challenging: money, time, or people? Which of these areas do you feel most comfortable administering?

3. How do you respond to overwhelming obstacles? Do you attack, withdraw, or are you paralyzed? What better responses should you consider?

CHAPTER SIX
THE PRINCIPLE OF GRATITUDE

Each summer, during orientation, I explained to the eager and excited high school and college-aged staff members that it was a privilege to serve the Lord at camp. I let them know from the start that I would not respond well to questions that began, *"Do we have to* _____*?"*

Camp ministry, like all service to the Lord, is an honor. Sure, we get tired, run down, bored, and exhausted. The grueling, relentless grind of summer takes its toll. But an attitude of gratitude goes a long way in helping us survive, and thrive, in the mundane and challenging phases of ministry.

Instead of *have to* we tried to insert the words *get to*. Do we *get to* clean the pool this evening? Do we *get to* wash all those pans of burnt lasagna? Do we *get to* mow the ballfield this afternoon?

It became a game with the staff, but words mean things. Life becomes what we say. Three decades later one staff member told me,

> We were consistently reminded that this was a 'Get to Summer.' We could teach the scriptures and sing all day long, but if we didn't serve our campers with an attitude of humility and service, then our words would ring hol-

> low. Many years later, our young family came to Family Camp. I smiled at the young staff members who carried my luggage, refilled our drink glasses, and loved on my babies all week. I hoped that they too would be forever changed by their "Get to Summer."

Another former staff member commented,

> It has served me well whenever I was tempted to complain or ask, 'Do I have to . . .?' It's a privilege and a joy to serve and love those around us in the name of Christ, especially your spouse, your children (even your adult children), or your aging parents. I'm grateful for this life lesson that I learned at camp, along with many other truths that transformed my life as a young believer.

Serving God, in the good times and bad, is always a privilege – a privilege for which we should always be thankful. If we truly see God's hand in the dirty dishes, homesick campers, and one more cabin clean-up challenge, we will serve with thankful hearts.

Jesus' heart of gratitude overflowed because he knew the ultimate Giver. God the Father provided exactly what everyone needed, at just the right time, and Jesus was grateful for his Father's compassionate and bountiful heart. Jesus knew his Father wanted the best for him, for the 5,000, and for the Twelve. Jesus knew that his Father had both the capacity to give and the compassion to provide for their needs. God's loving response flowed from the Father's character. Our role is to thank God for the opportunities to trust him and ask for his help, knowing that God will supply what we truly need.

As always, Jesus left us a powerful model of gratitude and its importance in camp ministry. Let's look at Jesus' grateful heart, how it influenced that day 2,000 years ago, and how it applies to camp ministry today.

Jesus' Grateful Heart

The problem – With 5,000 hungry *campers* getting restless, the Twelve Disciples may have engaged in a little finger pointing. *I knew this was a bad idea. You should have stopped him*! *You live around here; can't you do something?* Or maybe, *Who picked this campsite?*

Trying to shift responsibility is not unusual. No one likes to take the blame. When things go wrong, we look for someone to be the fall-guy. When things go well, we like to take the credit. We smugly think successful outcomes are obviously due to my skill, wisdom, hard work, courage, clever ideas, or giftedness. We all tend to take the credit when things are going well, but when the wheels come off, we generally point fingers and look for someone to blame.

Jesus did not take credit, nor did he show signs of despair, and he did not start pointing fingers at the Twelve. He merely recognized his role and played his part the way God intended. Jesus didn't fret, he was faithful. He wasn't traumatized, he was thankful.

From a human perspective the gift was not much, only a couple small fish and a few loaves of bread. Not much more than a small sandwich. But a generous little boy was willing to give what he had. Jesus appreciated both the small gift and the heart that offered it.

The Disciples' Dilemma – The disciples were captivated by two things. *First*, the meager resources available to them, and *second*, the massive crowd that needed to be fed. Their eyes darted between the massive crowd and the embarrassingly tiny lunch. One moment they were *overwhelmed* by the size

JESUS: CAMP DIRECTOR

of the crowd, *Look at all those people*! The next minute they were *underwhelmed* by the meager lunch available to them, *Look at this little lunch*! As the sun sank lower in the western sky the disciples stomachs were in knots, not because of hunger – but for lack of a solution. They had way too many people and way too little food. They could see the train wreck approaching and realized they could do nothing to stop it. Their unanimous opinion was – *this is sure to turn out badly*.

But Jesus viewed the situation differently than the disciples. He started the day surveying the crowd with eyes of compassion and he remained sensitive to their needs. But now his eyes moved from the gigantic crowd to the simple dinner menu – fish and bread – not much of a chef's special. But Jesus was neither concerned about the magnitude of the problem or the limited available resources. Instead of focusing his eyes on the huge crowd or the limited food supply, he *looked up*.

It's easy to look at a huge problem and be overwhelmed. The disciples did, and we do, too. Attendance is down, we need six more volunteers next week, the pool turned green, the cook just quit, and a major donor has pulled her support. Our problems are monumental, and if we stare at them they will stare back at us, bigger than life and smirking at our terror.

We stand stunned not knowing what to do or which way to turn. Shifting our attention, we look for anything to address our immense challenge – and all we find are a few fish and a little morsel of bread. Our bank account is overdrawn, our few friends are busy with their own problems, our schedule is packed with work, and kids, and parents, and . . . our souls are parched, and our hearts are downcast. We have nothing left to give. How will one small lunch of fish and loaves meet the massive needs and overwhelming problems that confront me?

Our eyes flit back and forth, first to the gigantic problem, then to the limited resources – the stack of bills and the empty checkbook. Back to the seemingly insurmountable challenge, then back to the seemingly insignificant resources. First the 5,000, then the fish and loaves, 5,000 and then the fish and loaves, 5,000 and then the fish and loaves. Where does our gaze land? On the *massive problem* or the *microscopic resources?*

As usual, Jesus had a better idea. Being aware of the very large problem and the very meager supply, Jesus realized he had a powerful teaching opportunity. He taught the crowd, the disciples, and *us* a fundamental life lesson, *when everything around us is bleak, look up!* When crushing problems surround us, when we have little or no resources to sustain us, *look up!*

> *Jesus was neither concerned about the magnitude of the problem or the limited available resources. Instead of focusing his eyes on the huge crowd or the limited food supply, he looked up.*

Gratitude Begins When We Look Up. Looking up does four things. *First*, we divert our attention away from the insurmountable problem and meager resources. *Second*, we acknowledge that we are at the end of our rope; we need help, we cannot do this alone. *Third*, we recognize that God alone is our strength, wisdom, courage, and peace. And *fourth*, we regain our spiritual and emotional equilibrium. We are reminded that God is on his thrown and He remains sovereign over all.

When we focus on the problem we will always be defeated. None of us has the strength and stamina to go head-to-head with life's challenges and win.

But looking up was not the only thing that Jesus did. He also *gave thanks*! I'm sure Jesus gave thanks for the crowd who had listened to him share the good news of God's Kingdom. He probably gave thanks for the people who had been healed and the little boy whose lunch had been offered. And I think he gave thanks for the teachable moment in the lives of his disciples. There were many things on the *thank-you* list, but for the disciples those items of thanks had been overshadowed by the gigantic problem that captured and held their attention.

Too often the trauma and drama of the moment calls our attention to the painful experiences in our lives, and we miss all beauty and grace around us.

Giving thanks should come easily for those who work in camp ministry.

If we stop and reflect, we can always come up with a list of reasons to give thanks. Each morning my wife and I pray for family and friends and circumstances that are on our hearts. But we always start with each of us expressing gratitude for five things that we are thankful for: an encouraging phone call, a beautiful sunrise, a new friendship, a powerful sermon, a picture from a grandchild, an answered prayer, or any number of blessings. The list reminds us of the good things God provides and resets our hearts to a default of gratitude.

Life is tough. Being grateful for God's grace does not mean that tough times will not overtake us. And when those bilious clouds roll in, it is easy to forget the good things that God has done for us. Joseph interpreted a troubling dream for Pharaoh that had two parts. In the first segment seven beautiful, large, healthy cows enjoyed an afternoon grazing along the lush Nile River. Then seven skinny, scrawny, sickly cows came along and gobbled them up, and afterward they looked just as bad as before their meal. The second half is a similar story, but this time it is heads of grain. Seven beautiful heads of grain waved in the breeze – along came seven withered heads of grain that consumed the healthy ones, yet the emaciated heads of grain remained gaunt. The story is about seven abundant years followed by seven years of famine, but the principle for us is that good times always give way to bad times. When the bad times come, they not only bring their miserable presence, tilting life's balance with more bad than good, they try to demolish and destroy the good years that we have enjoyed – if we let them.

We quickly forget the good things in our lives when tough times arrive. The enjoyment of good health that we took for granted is gone when disease gobbles it up. The security of a regular income is gone when we lose our job. The warmth of a loving relationship is gone when we are abandoned. As circumstances shift, so can the gratitude of our hearts. We become consumed by our current misery and quickly forget the good times and joy of the past.

Even in our best moments we must be careful. Our grateful hearts can easily be subverted in two ways: *first*, we can fail to express gratitude by taking our health, jobs, and relationships for granted. We can fail to show appreciation for the seven fat cows and seven healthy grains God brings into our lives. Or *second*, we may grumble about what is gone. We quickly become disgruntled and angry when areas of peace, joy, satisfaction, or support are removed. Either way we fail to give thanks.

Giving thanks should come easily for those who work in camp ministry. We get to live and work in beautiful places, we meet interesting people, our days are never boring, we make life-long friends, many of us are paid to serve God, and we wave goodbye to our mistakes after only a few days. Life could be worse. However, instead of appreciating the gift and thanking the giver, we tend to focus on the massive challenges and fret about the lack of resources.

Like Jesus, we need to be aware of the significant needs in the crowd around us. We are to hold our resources gently in our hands and then look up to the One who works miracles. Only then can we thank him for what he has provided and trust him to multiply our efforts for his glory. The outcome may not look exactly the way we expected, but God honors grateful hearts and will do great things with the little we have when we apply the *Principle of Gratitude*.

THE PRINCIPLE OF GRATITUDE

Discussion Questions

1. What is your camp grateful for today? Create a *Grateful to God* list of at least 10 things for which your camp can thank God.

2. Think of a difficult challenge that your camp has faced in the past few years. What blessings do you now see, looking back on that event?

3. What challenge is your camp facing today? What can you be thankful for despite today's uncomfortable circumstances?

Personal Reflections

1. It is not easy to be grateful for all of life's events. What are some situations in your past that remain difficult to thank God for?

2. Reflect on your past five years. What are one or two things you are thankful for that occurred in each of these years? What does this tell you about God's faithfulness?

3. Who are you grateful for? Give them a call, write them a note, or offer a prayer of gratitude for them.

CHAPTER SEVEN
THE PRINCIPLE OF STRATEGIC PROGRAMMING

Camp programming can take many forms, some more effective than others. Each camp is unique, and each camp designs its time and activities the right way – *for them*. Good programming involves purposely designing each activity of camp to help achieve the desired result(s). The more clearly articulated the outcome(s) of camp, the more intentionally the program can be designed. *Purpose* must direct *practice*.

Until a person or institution knows where it wants to go, any road will suffice. Without a clearly defined end, all pathways are equally helpful – or harmful.

Some camps pattern their program after the competitor on the other side of the lake, or the camp they envy on the other side of the country. What they see are the fun games, busy schedule, exciting activities, and creative experiences. *Wow, we need that whiz bag, super-duper, gotta-have, fun thing* is their first response. Maybe they do need it, or maybe they don't.

When a camp designs its program based upon available options, it forfeits the opportunity to be strategic. By starting with a collection of available alternatives, a camp will create a box full of unstrung pearls, lots of beautiful pieces but lacking any essential strategic connection.

Starting with a strong cord woven from theological, philosophic, and contextualized threads will determine which pearls will be added and in what sequence. The string is rarely seen but that critical fiber runs through the entire strand providing the essential connection that makes camp programming beautiful and valuable.

Some camps emphasize the relational aspect of the experience and focus on small group interactions. This style is often called *decentralized* or *counselor-centered* camping. Others are committed to powerful platform presentations and large group events. This style is generally referred to as *centralized* or *speaker-centered* camping (or by its critics, *church-in-the-woods*). Many find a third way, combining these two contrasting methods to develop a hybrid style of camp. Hybrid camping utilizes the strong relational emphasis of decentralized camping and the powerful content delivery of centralized camping. Hybrid camping draws on the strength of each style, but also must face the challenges that limit the effectiveness of both. Any of these styles can work well, depending on what the camp hopes to accomplish.

> His ability to present well on the platform and his facilitation of follow-up discussion did not limit his ability to interact personally with some of those in attendance.

Jesus adapted his style and embraced numerous forms of ministry as he programmed his massive day-camp. He used a centralized approach as he spoke to 5,000 people. He had no microphone, no sound system, no audio-visual support; he just spoke with clarity, challenge, power, and authority. The people were enthralled by his message. Jesus controlled the accuracy and content of his presentation and

THE PRINCIPLE OF STRATEGIC PROGRAMMING

he ensured that his truth was communicated well. He knew how to do *church-in-the-woods* and he did it powerfully and effectively.

Later, he divided the mass of humanity into small groups of between 50 and 100. The small groups certainly did more than facilitate the distribution of the meal. The small groups allowed for discussion, interaction, follow-up dialogue, and questions. Jesus' presentation had been a wonderful one-way delivery of exquisite truth, but people needed an opportunity to process what they had heard and engage with it personally and relationally. The small groups provided that opportunity.

Along the way, Jesus healed individuals, chatted with a generous young boy, and interacted with several of his disciples. His ability to present well on the platform and his facilitation of follow-up discussion did not limit his ability to interact personally with some of those in attendance.

The healing service was most likely very personal. Those struggling with infirmities, physical hardships, diseases, mental health issues, and demonic oppression were not lumped in a corner and shouted at from a distance. The line may have formed, or a crowd encircled him, but Jesus addressed those with special needs and painful burdens in very personal ways.

What makes good programming? What should influence a camp's decision-making as it struggles to find the best way to serve its campers and guests? The answer will depend on what the camp is trying to accomplish and the context within which it operates.

Strategic programming engages every aspect of camp. It is woven into the entire fabric of the experience and permeates every decision that affects the camp. Let's explore a few key areas: education, recreation, and food service.

Education

A large part of camp involves education. Bible study, sports training, life-skills acquisition, and social development are all parts of the education experience that many camps provide. Camp programming generally falls into one of three styles: centralized, decentralized, or hybrid. And a fourth, experiential education, is similar to the decentralized model.

Centralized - Camps that are primarily concerned about content, ones that want to ensure that their message is clean, accurate, and consistent, will probably utilize a centralized approach. One strong teacher will communicate a clear message powerfully and precisely. This centralized approach is highly effective for content delivery, but it has its drawbacks. In a large crowd, campers can hide in plain sight, information can be heard but not engaged, and personalized application can be avoided. The strength of centralized camping is the ability to communicate truth clearly and effectively. The weakness is whether any of that truth will be applied in a camper's life.

Decentralized - Camps that focus on relationships utilize a different approach. Small group leaders facilitate interactive discussions. Bible studies focus on discovering truth. Questions are entertained and answers explored. But it takes a large team of highly skilled and well-trained small-group leaders to make this style of camp successful. Chances increase that information will not be shared accurately, and that errors, misunderstanding, and misrepresentations will creep into the conversations. When done well, decentralized camping is highly effective, but the staffing challenges are significant.

THE PRINCIPLE OF STRATEGIC PROGRAMMING

Hybrid - Hybrid camp programs adopt the best of both options, and they assume the liabilities associated with each model. In real life, most camps use a hybrid approach, however, they tend to lean to one end of the continuum or the other. They adjust their educational design to adapt to the challenges that come with their programmatic selections.

Experiential Education – Centralized, decentralized, and hybrid styles of camp generally build their educational framework around learning God's Word and applying it to life. Another style, much like decentralized camp programming, is experiential education. This method starts with life events and applies God's truth to critical moments of self-awareness. The leadership staff begin the process by briefing the campers about the challenges ahead. Sometimes these are natural events such as a canoe trip or backpacking adventure, but often these are created and controlled challenges like a climbing wall or ropes course. During and after the event, the leadership staff probe and challenge the participants to understand what is happening to them and the group.

The physical, emotional, relational, and spiritual challenges are then explored to see what God's Word says to these exhilarating, perplexing, and sometimes disturbing events. Healthy debriefing exercises help campers explore the new insights derived from the evaluated experience. The training and preparation of the staff to execute this level of engagement is significant. Both the skill level needed for the activity and the safety training in preparation for the adventure are critical. The ability to effectively conduct the evaluation and debriefing exercises that follow each event is also critically important.

JESUS: CAMP DIRECTOR

Most camps follow Jesus' example and try to create multiple methods of educational engagement. They strive to create programs that touch the lives of people in a variety of ways. Most camps provide some type of large group presentations, Bible studies, prayer meetings, story times, firesides, and seminars that deliver forums for information to be clearly disseminated. They also design small group discussions that enable staff leaders to engage campers with the biblical content, address questions, and dig deeper. Camp activities and adventures create an amazing context for experiential learning. Time for debriefing and extended processing of experiences occurs naturally at camp. Great camp experiences blend multiple teaching methods to reach a diverse group of campers – just like Jesus did!

Recreation

Recreation, whether active or passive, should also be built around the camp's program philosophy. Does the camp want active recreation with go-carts racing through the camp creating energy and excitement, or does it want passive recreation with isolated benches overlooking a tranquil lake for reflection and conversations? Both can be right and both can be wrong, depending on the desired outcome(s). High energy activities or quiet contemplation can both provide valuable outcomes for campers, depending on the results the camp is striving to achieve.

Recreational programming can be competitive or cooperative. In one camp, teams may compete to memorize the most Bible verses, clean and decorate their cabins, show the most spirit, or clear their dinner table the fastest. But at the camp down the road, campers may work together to build a raft, dramatically present a Bible story, learn responsible creation care skills, or prepare for a choir presentation.

Which is right? Both or neither, depending on how aligned their practices are with the camp's stated purposes.

> *Great camp experiences blend multiple teaching methods to reach a diverse group of campers – just like Jesus did!*

Food Service

Even the nitty-gritty operational elements of camp, like food service, should be directed by a philosophy of ministry. Why do camps serve meals as they do? Is the driving goal to control costs or to create an effective context for ministry? Do we use round tables or ones with a rectangular design? Open seating or in cabin groups? Carpet, tile, or cement floors? Cafeteria, buffet, banquet, or family-style serving? Do the campers clean-up after meals, or is that the staff's responsibility? Is mealtime a chance to rest and refill, or an opportunity to relax and engage in significant conversations? Again, there are no right or wrong answers. Food service styles are not ethically good or bad. However, some choices are more congruent with a desired outcome, therefore the decisions about food service, like all aspects of camp, should reflect the philosophic foundation of the ministry.

Whether the programming decisions involve education, recreation, food service, or other aspects of camp, the core decisions rest on considerations of spiritual impact. What is the primary outcome desired by the camp? Camps generally emphasize one of four basic spiritual results, but almost every camp deals with all four: 1) evangelism, 2) discipleship, 3) leadership development, or 4) recovery. At its core, the Great Commission involves making disciples.

The controlling verb in the sentence is *matheteusate* which simply means **to make disciples**. *Then Jesus came to them and said, "All authority in heaven and on earth has been given to me. Therefore go and make disciples of all nations, baptizing them in the name of the Father and of the Son and of the Holy Spirit, and teaching them to obey everything I have commanded you. And surely I am with you always, to the very end of the age"* (Matthew 28:20).

Baptizing them speaks to the entry into God's family. That happens a lot at camp and many camps make evangelism their primary emphasis.

Teaching them to observe all things speaks to at least three related outcomes.

- *First*, it can be applied to basic spiritual development. Many camps strive to help campers deepen their commitments to walk with God and obey his commands and make this their top priority.
- *Second*, leadership development can be in play. Some camps see their primary objective as developing and training the next generation of spiritual leaders.
- *Third*, other camps are designed to help those whose lives have been shattered by their own sinful choices or the devastating behaviors of others.

In the real world of camp ministry, there is immense adaptability and camps engage campers where they are, providing whatever help is needed. Camps are eager to furnish the spiritual assistance needed to start, grow, develop, or reengage each camper's walk with Jesus.

So, what is the optimal programming methodology for camp ministry? Like Jesus, camping leaders must be flexible and adaptable. They must determine what style of programming will be most effective in achieving their spiritual goals. And they must adapt to the needs of the guests and apply the *Principle of Strategic Programming.*

 *Discussion Questions*

1. Would you describe your camp's program strategy as centralized, decentralized, or hybrid? How do the activities and operations of your camp align with this program strategy?

2. What are some of the biggest challenges you face while employing your chosen program strategy?

3. How does your camp's style of food service support or detract from your chosen program strategy?

Personal Reflections

1. What do you enjoy most about ministry: evangelism, encouraging Christian growth, leadership development, or helping people recover from difficult circumstances?

2. What style of camp ministry best matches your gifts: centralized, decentralized, or hybrid? Why do you think this is true?

3. Do you tend to begin planning by considering options that are available to you, or by articulating your purpose, goals, and desired outcomes? Is this something you should adjust?

CHAPTER EIGHT
THE PRINCIPLE OF STEWARDSHIP

Like most homes, we have a jar full of pennies. We toss loose change into a bowl and eventually recover the silvery ones for the parking meter or vending machine, but what about all those pennies? Because there are so many of them, they hold little value. But in 1955, an error in the Philadelphia mint generated just over 20,000 of these little copper coins that were struck twice, marring them, and giving them an unusual appearance. Most were recovered and destroyed but some made their way into circulation. Oddly, that flaw generated immense value. Because there are only a few of them, some of those pennies have sold for over $50,000. The abundance of common pennies leaves them hardly worth stooping down to pick one off the street. But the scarcity of a similar yet slightly disfigured coin creates extreme value.

We value what is in short supply, but disregard things in abundance. We crave what we do not have and disdain the common. In two ways, this human tendency threatens our God-given charge to be good stewards of what he has entrusted to us. *First*, we give undo importance to things we lack. And *second*, we become negligent with what we have in abundance. We *overvalue what is scarce* and *undervalue what is ordinary.*

When we have plenty of water, we don't think twice about letting the leaky faucet drip. When we have unlimited trees, we don't fret about cutting them down. When there is a sea full of fish, we are comfortable catching all we can. Only when scarcity becomes real do we begin to value what is ebbing away.

> *As Christians we are not motivated by fear, but instead, by our desire to please the One who entrusted this world to us.*

On that grassy hillside two-thousand years ago, a large throng of people needed food. The only resource available was a small lunch with a few loaves of bread and a couple of small fish. The little boy could have garnered a small fortune scalping his lunch to the highest bidder. Scarcity made it valuable. But after the people were well-fed and their hunger assuaged, there were 12 baskets that they could not give away.

After the meal, 5,000 guests were stuffed and the Twelve collected 12 baskets of leftovers. Jesus directed them, *Gather the pieces that are left over. Let nothing be wasted* (John 6:12). Jesus looked past the scarcity and abundance issues and recognized the intrinsic value in the leftover food – and the incalculable worth of each person in the well-fed crowd. Camping leaders are tasked with caring for both the resources entrusted to us and the people we encounter along the way. *Let nothing be wasted!*

There are at least three areas in which Christian camping leaders should follow Christ's example and *let nothing be wasted. First,* camps should not waste the magnificent, created environment where camps reside. *Second,* camps should not waste the valuable resources entrusted to them. And *third*, camps should not waste the ministry opportunities that abound within them.

Caring for God's Creation

Christian camping leaders should set the standard in caring for God's creation. However, the motivation for these actions may be quite different from the reasons voiced by the world. As Christian stewards, we do not protect and care for forests, flowers, fish, fowl, and fauna because it took millions of years of chance and good fortune for them to appear. We are not afraid that the world will collapse if we fail to act or worry that cataclysmic events will happen on our watch. Nor do we feel guilty because we happened to have advanced a step ahead of other species. We do not strive to be good stewards because things are getting out of control. Quite the contrary. We care for the earth and all that is in it because God has graciously given us that privilege and responsibility.

Real problems exist. Many are caused by the choices that we and our ancestors have made. However, we move forward in this broken world with the assurance that God's ability to redeem is greater than our capacity to ruin, and his sovereignty will always overwhelm our selfishness. As Christians we are not motivated by fear, but instead, by our desire to please the One who entrusted this world to us.

Christian camps hold a unique role within the various ministries God has established. Since the outdoor setting is an essential component of camp ministry, Christian camping leaders should model a high degree of care for the world God has entrusted to us.[2] We hold a mandate from God to rule over and care for the Garden into which he has placed us. Sin's impact marred mankind and the ground.

The pervasive and onerous consequences of sin make our job exponentially more difficult. Our sinful tendencies move us toward selfish and exploitative behaviors. We tend to think only of ourselves and act in not-so-benevolent self-interests, often at the expense of those around us and those who come after us. Additionally, the ground has been cursed leaving it susceptible to thorns and thistles and vulnerable to decay and corruption. Caring for God's creation is not easy, but it is critical, especially in an era when the world is highly sensitive to environmental issues.

Our care for the world is based upon our calling and our commitment to fulfill the mandate God has entrusted to us. God has deputized us to superintend the world and has given us authority to rule over it for better – not for worse. Camp gardens, recycling commitments, non-intrusive architectural design, and a general mindset of sensitivity to God's creation are all significant to authentic Christian camping ministry. *Let nothing go to waste.*

Caring for God's Resources

Camps accumulate stuff! Residential camps require land, buildings, roads, food service equipment, vehicles, water systems, computers, maintenance tools, fences, recreational equipment, and maybe some horses. Adventure camps have it a little easier. A few canoes, backpacks, tents, climbing ropes, helmets, cooking equipment, and maybe a van or bus. Oh yes, a storage building and an office with a computer or two. No matter what style of camping ministry is involved, it is equipment intensive. Ownership requires care and oversight of the land, buildings, and equipment entrusted to Christian camps.

As responsible stewards we are to *let nothing be wasted.* That means preserving buildings, repairing vehicles, storing equipment, and maintaining supplies. Responsible care of what God has entrusted to us comes with the leadership territory.

Sacrificial gifts are often the source of the *stuff* of camps. Funds used to purchase land, build buildings, or buy equipment may come from fees charged for camp or sacrificial contributions. Whatever the source, leaders must remember that the money remains the Lord's and stewardship is a sacred responsibility. Camps carry a responsibility to their donors and to the Lord to ensure that *nothing is wasted*.

Care of the Opportunities God Provides

Let's look at the story once again. When everyone had eaten their fill, Jesus instructed the disciples to collect the leftovers. He said, *let nothing be wasted*. Jesus was concerned that the abundance he had created not be wasted. Just because supply outstripped demand did not diminish the intrinsic value of the food. The small lunch of bread and fish that had been in short supply an hour earlier could have fetched a small fortune. Now, with Jesus' powerful and abundant provision, everyone was satisfied, and no one was interested in the leftovers.

As usual, Jesus had a better idea. He wanted everything he created to be treated with respect and fully utilized. Just because the food was abundantly available did not diminish its significance. Twelve baskets of food were not to be discarded just because the people had eaten their full. The food, like everything and everyone Jesus created, was designed for a purpose and was worthy of respect.

The stakes, however, were much higher than a few baskets of leftovers. His command to scoop up the leftover crusts and to salvage a few morsels of fish was also a picture of things to come. Once again, Jesus was looking a little farther down the road.

Mark records two great feedings – one with 4,000 and the other, that Matthew, Luke, and John also record, fed 5,000 hungry mouths. When the 5,000 were fed, the disciples collected 12 baskets of remnants. But when Jesus fed the 4,000, seven baskets of scraps were salvaged.

Jesus used the disciples' lack of understanding about these two great feedings to lead them into a deeper discussion and fuller awareness of a critical spiritual truth.

By any standards, feeding 4,000 people as an encore to feeding 5,000 is a first-class miracle (Mark 8:1-9a). But this second massive feeding was followed by an awkward encounter with a group of religious leaders who demanded a sign from heaven to validate Jesus' authority – and possibly to provide them with another free lunch! Jesus' response is classic – he *sighed deeply*. My mother used to sigh deeply, with her hands on her hips as she shook her head and thought not quite out loud, *what am I going to do with this boy?* Jesus follows his exasperated sigh with a sharp rebuke of the religious leaders and a quick departure by boat across the Sea of Galilee (Mark 8:9b-13).

As Jesus and the disciples climb back into the boat, Mark notes a tactical error. As they set sail, they forgot to pack a sufficient lunch. They only had one loaf of bread with them – to divide between thirteen hungry sailors (Mark 8:14).

We do not know what happened to the rest of the seven baskets. They may have been given to the poor, distributed to other followers, or enough time may have elapsed for the group to have finished off the baskets themselves. Whatever transpired, the food was gone, and the miracle forgotten.

Coming off the encounter with the religious leaders, and not wanting to waste a teaching opportunity, Jesus addressed his disciples. *"Be careful," Jesus warned them. "Watch out for the yeast of the Pharisees and that of Herod"* (Mark 8:15). Yeast is almost always used as a negative object lesson describing sin's ability to infiltrate every aspect of a person's life, infecting it in a debilitating way. Yeast changes the very nature of dough – as sin does our souls.

In the back of the boat, one hungry disciple whispered to another, *he is tormenting us with a food illustration because we don't have anything to eat* (my paraphrase). Mark records the comments:

> *The disciples had forgotten to bring bread, except for one loaf they had with them in the boat. "Be careful," Jesus warned them. "Watch out for the yeast of the Pharisees and that of Herod." They discussed this with one another and said, "It is because we have no bread."* (Mark 8:14-16)

Once again, Jesus, not wanting to waste an opportunity to make a significant point, seized the teachable moment. Mark continues,

> *Aware of their discussion, Jesus asked them: "Why are you talking about having no bread? Do you still not see or understand? Are your hearts hardened? Do you have eyes but fail to see, and ears but fail to hear? And don't you remember? When I broke the five loaves for the five thousand, how many basketfuls of pieces did you pick up?" "Twelve," they replied. "And when I broke the seven loaves for the four thousand, how many basketfuls of pieces did you pick up?" They answered, "Seven." He said to them, "Do you still not understand?"* (Mark 8:17-21)

Do you still not understand what? What is it that Jesus wanted the disciples to understand? Jesus used the disciples' lack of understanding about these two great feedings to lead them into a deeper discussion and fuller awareness of a critical spiritual truth. The next two events include a two-phased healing of a blind man in Bethsaida and a discussion on the road to Caesarea Philippi. As we will see, Jesus does not waste these moments either.

Bethsaida was the closest town to where the feeding of the 5,000 took place, and the hometown of at least a third of the disciples. Jesus took the man outside the city and used a medical procedure probably not approved anywhere today. The miracle was completed in two steps. *First*, the man's sight improved from absolute darkness to the ability to distinguish light and blurred images. *Second*, Jesus completely restored the man's sight, allowing him to see everything clearly.

Jesus did not err or fail to use enough supernatural power the first time he addressed the man's need. Jesus healed the man in two phases as an object lesson to demonstrate the spiritual condition of the disciples. They had moved from darkness to light, they understood that they were following an amazing rabbi and world-class prophet. But things were still a little blurry, now they needed clarity. They needed to see Jesus for who he truly was.

The story continued. They left Bethsaida and headed north making the 20-mile hike to Caesarea Philippi. Along the way they walked and talked, looked at the surrounding countryside, and reflected on the amazing events of the previous days. Then Jesus, not wanting to waste the moment, redirected the conversation with a rather innocuous question: *What's the word on the streets? What did you hear back in Bethsaida? Who do people think I am?*

THE PRINCIPLE OF STEWARDSHIP

> *When Jesus came to the region of Caesarea Philippi, he asked his disciples, "Who do people say the Son of Man is?" They replied, "Some say John the Baptist; others say Elijah; and still others, Jeremiah or one of the prophets."* (Matthew 16:14)

The disciples probably laughed as they shared the funny speculations they had overheard in Bethsaida. One reported, *I heard a guy in the butcher shop say that you are John the Baptist. No way*! They all laughed. Another chimed in, *A guy at the bakery said you are Elijah back from the dead*. Again, uproarious laughter. Another said, *A friend of mine is sure you are Jeremiah*, as the group shook their heads wondering how people could be so foolish! Those silly people back in Bethsaida, how could they think such things?

Once the disciples had identified who Jesus was *not*, he sprung the trap. No longer was Jesus interested in what others speculated, instead he made the conversation personal. *What about you? Who do you guys think I am?*

The sound of the sandals on the pathway became very loud as a hush fell over the group. Their minds race to feedings, healings, miracles, and teachings. Peter could not abide the silence and spoke for himself, and the group:

> *"But what about you?" he asked. "Who do you say I am?" Simon Peter answered, "You are the Christ, the Son of the living God." Jesus replied, "Blessed are you, Simon son of Jonah, for this was not revealed to you by man, but by my Father in heaven."* (Matthew 16:15-17)

Their sight had gone from blurry speculation to crystal clear perception. Their rabbi was the Messiah.

JESUS: CAMP DIRECTOR

Christian camping leaders follow Jesus' example when they *let nothing be wasted*. Wise leaders strive to make their camps *waste-free* environments. They set the example as good stewards of God's creation, and care deeply for the resources God has entrusted to them. But most of all, they ensure that ministry opportunities are not wasted. Teachable moments occur during hikes, between games, after meetings, while cleaning the cabin, and in small group conversations. Great camp leaders do not waste opportunities when campers are ready to wrestle with spiritual truth or waste opportunities for campers and staff to make life-changing and eternity-altering decisions. They consistently apply the *Principle of Stewardship*.

THE PRINCIPLE OF STEWARDSHIP

Discussion Questions

1. What are some things your camp has in abundance? *(These could be physical materials, skills, gifts, or any other resources.)* Do you take any of these for granted?

2. In what ways is your camp being a good steward of its physical resources? In what areas could it improve?

3. In what ways is your camp being a good steward of its spiritual giftedness, strengths, and heritage? In what ways could this stewardship be improved?

Personal Reflections

1. What gifts do you feel you have been given? How are you using and developing these gifts?

2. What more can you do to be a good steward of the earth? What motivates you to be a good steward? How might your motivation be similar or dissimilar to the motivations of others?

3. What are you doing to be a responsible, spiritual steward and to utilize the things you have learned at camp?

CHAPTER NINE
THE PRINCIPLE OF DUAL IMPACT

The massive, powerful, outspoken former professional athlete was an imposing figure. His handshake alone intimidated me as his enormous paw engulfed mine. During his playing-days, he amassed a small fortune and a stunning array of serious injuries. Now he invested his time, money, and influence operating a Christian camp.

He began our conversation – or his monologue – extolling the virtues of his camp and explaining the uniqueness of his ministry. Besides a strong sports emphasis, he was adamant that camp was *not* about the campers. The heart of his camp ministry was developing his college-age *staff members* into godly, strong, and effective leaders.

To each his own, I thought to myself, not wanting to pick a fight with a man who knocked people down for a living. But my perspective was radically different. Helping develop staff was a fine by-product and a necessary part of the big picture, but only a sideshow in the focused ministry of serving campers. From my perspective, camp was all about the campers, pure and simple. If others benefited, wonderful, just do not distract camp from its ultimate goal of serving campers and guests.

JESUS: CAMP DIRECTOR

So, two camps, two programs, two directors, two philosophies, and two purposes – serving campers or developing staff, which should take priority? My massive colleague had his ideas, and I had mine. We were both right – and both wrong.

> *Every camper should be welcomed and greeted with warmth, love, and respect. As they arrive, they should feel that they are entering a safe zone, a haven of love, security, and acceptance.*

What was Jesus' emphasis? Was he focused on the twelve intern-like disciples, or was he committed to meeting the needs of his 5,000 camper-like listeners? Jesus showed little interest in the classifications or labels attached to the people. The tags *camper* or *staff* were rather inconsequential to his ministry. He seemed to rise above the labels and see people as individuals with specific and unique needs. Jesus approached each person individually with spiritual goals for everyone he encountered – *campers* and *staff*. But he did approach the Twelve differently than the throng. He expressed general, yet intentional, ministry plans for his 5,000 *campers*, and he employed focused, developmental objectives for his twelve *interns*.

Ministry to the 5,000 Campers

Luke summarizes Jesus' ministry to the 5,000 simply and well, *He welcomed them and spoke to them about the Kingdom of God and healed those who needed healing* (Luke 9:11). Jesus' ministry to the large crowd of *campers* appears broad and applicable to all. In a large camp setting, leaders must find general themes that will provide help and direction to the largest number of campers. The *campers*

Jesus met needed at least three types of ministries: 1) acceptance, 2) teaching, and 3) healing. And eventually, they all needed to eat! Those same needs accompany campers who attend Christian camps today.

Welcome and Acceptance

Jesus' ministry to the multitude began with a welcoming attitude of acceptance. Luke records Jesus' attitude as he first engaged the crowd: *Jesus welcomed them* (Luke 9:11a). Whatever else camp might be, it should be an emotionally safe and secure place of acceptance. Due to today's incessant social media activity and aggressive communication practices, many young people face intense peer rejection and public shaming like no generation before them. Family breakdowns, frequent moves, financial pressures, social unrest, political turmoil, and shifting cultural norms all play into the fears, threats, and isolation that young people feel today.

Each camper is made in the image of God. This image is not related to strength, beauty, skin color, hair color, height, weight, parents' wealth, status, skills, or zip code. Though marred by sin, God's image is etched on individual hearts. Every camper should be welcomed and greeted with warmth, love, and respect. As they arrive, they should feel that they are entering a *safe zone*, a haven of love, security, and acceptance.

Acceptance is a critical foundation for ministry, but our acts of love for campers must not be a ploy designed merely to lead them to a new level of trust for the camp's benefit. Acceptance is not a cleverly contrived strategy to entice campers to *our way* of thinking or to accept *our* system of belief. As much as we want that to happen, each camper is worthy of our acceptance and respect because of God's imprint on his or her life. As we grasp our own unworthiness and simultaneously glimpse how much God loves us, we can begin to extend love to those around us who are also fraught with scars, weakness, failures, and selfishness. We must accept and love others as Christ loved us. And camp is a wonderful place to learn and practice acceptance. Genuine love will pave the pathway to authentic spiritual conversations.

A warm welcome is essential but insufficient. A*cceptance* must be accompanied by *instruction*. The welcome, on the hillside in Galilee, soon flowed into a time of teaching. The content of what Jesus' taught his 5,000 *campers* was only captured in summary. We do not know the details of his message. Mark gives us a tiny glimpse, *When Jesus landed and saw a large crowd, he had compassion on them, because they were like sheep without a shepherd. So he began teaching them many things* (Mark 6:34). *Many things?* Mark could not have been less helpful. What *many things?* What topics? What content? What details?

> *Genuine love will pave the pathway to authentic spiritual conversations.*

Luke provides a little more insight, but not much. *He welcomed them and spoke to them about the kingdom of God, and healed those who needed healing* (Luke 9:11). At least we know that Jesus' topic was the Kingdom of God.

Speculating on the content of Jesus' teaching would be dangerous and unfair to the Gospel writers. The authors would have included more detail if it was relevant to their arguments. Apparently, knowing that Jesus taught them *many things* about the Kingdom of God is all we need to know. What we do know is that following the warm, compassionate greeting – content mattered. The large group received quality input and a significant message. They were taught *many things* that Jesus deemed important for them to know, and his message centered around the Kingdom of God. The campers all heard the same message, general, clear, basic, powerful, and consistent.

Jesus' plan for ministry was not exclusively for himself and his 12 interns, he engaged some of the 5,000 as well. The little boy gave his lunch. At least a dozen people supplied the 12 baskets used to collect the leftovers. And others must have aided those needing healing as they struggled to reach Jesus. Ministry at camp often calls for wise engagement of our guests as they bring knowledge, skills, and experience that can help others. Opportunities for them to participate in ministry should be readily available.

Jesus reached out to a few in the crowd with a personal touch. He engaged some people who came with specific needs, he interacted personally with a little boy who offered his lunch, and he prompted others to help in the work. However, most of the 5,000 received teaching and benefited from a ministry that was one-way communication. Jesus spoke, they listened. The truth of God was clearly presented by Jesus himself, the Way, the Truth, and the Life.

Campers were the focus of Jesus' acceptance and teaching, but staff and individuals needed Jesus' attention as well.

Ministry to His Staff Members

As much as he relished the opportunity to welcome and teach the crowd, and to interact with a few in personal ways, Jesus also worked in very pointed and personal ways with the people closest to him. He knew that his disciples were tired, disappointed, and ready to see the long day come to an end. But Jesus had additional challenges for all of them as they organized, fed, and cleaned up after the massive crowd. Jesus taught and trained his disciples by involving them in the work.

All the disciples participated in the ministry by dividing the crowd into smaller groups, they helped distribute the fish and bread, and it is no surprise that *twelve* baskets were needed to collect the leftovers! Jesus engaged each of his team members in the work of the ministry. He knew that they would learn best by participating, not just observing.

Jesus targeted at least one of his staff members, Philip, with a special opportunity for accelerated learning and growth. John provides this glimpse into the story and shows how Jesus approached Philip with a special challenge.

> *When Jesus looked up and saw a great crowd coming toward him, he said to Philip, "Where shall we buy bread for these people to eat?" He asked this only to test him, for he already had in mind what he was going to do. Philip answered him, "Eight months' wages would not buy enough bread for each one to have a bite!"* (John 6:5-7)

Philip lived in the area. That may have been why Jesus singled him out to deal with the food service challenge.[3] Philip's neighbors, friends, acquaintances, and possibly family members may have joined the throng that gathered that day. Being a part of Jesus' inner circle probably set Philip apart from the other locals of his generation who were now fishermen, farmers, shepherds, and shopkeepers. He may have enjoyed the moment a little too much and might have needed some air let out of his balloon. Or possibly, Jesus wanted to encourage him by giving him the first opportunity to recognize that this overwhelming need could not be met without supernatural involvement. Philip was offered the opportunity to ask Jesus for divine intervention. Jesus' approach to Philip was not random, his question was not just because Philip may have been standing nearby. John is very clear, this question was a targeted test, an unexpected *pop quiz*.

Philip failed the test, but he did not fail the course. Jesus seemed to take Philip's frustrated, short-sighted, natural response in stride, and flowed smoothly into an interaction with a little boy who placed his meager lunch into Jesus' hands. Philip, like the other disciples, needed to learn the critical lesson of how to deal with life's insurmountable challenges and unresolvable problems. He would always be overwhelmed until he truly understood who Jesus was and relied on him for the supernatural strength and wisdom he needed.

Yes, camp is for the campers. Yes, camp is for the staff.

Jesus engaged the 5,000 with compassionate acceptance, clearly shared significant truth, and healed those with specific needs. But all the while he engaged the Twelve, testing them and challenging them. Jesus' approach was not to humiliate or embarrass them but to develop their ministry skills and deepen their awareness of who he was. Yes, camp is for people! People whom Jesus welcomed, people whom Jesus taught, and people whom Jesus healed. And camp is for people who need greater ministry skills and a deeper understanding of who God is as they prepare to face ministry challenges in the days ahead. Jesus consistently and lovingly applied the *Principle of Dual Impact!*

JESUS: CAMP DIRECTOR

Discussion Questions

1. Who receives the primary ministry focus of your camp: staff/volunteers, campers, or both? Is this focus intentional or has it just evolved?

2. What can your camp do to better serve its staff/volunteers before, during, and after camp?

3. What can your camp do to better serve its campers, before, during, and after camp?

Personal Reflections

1. What influenced your life more, your time as a camper or as a staff member? Why do you think this is so?

2. Think of a person who ministered to you as a camper and another as a staff member? What made each of them influential in your life?

3. Which do you enjoy most, ministry to staff/volunteers or campers?

4. Do you receive more positive feedback from your ministry to the staff/volunteers or your ministry to campers?

CHAPTER TEN
THE PRINCIPLE OF THE BIG BODY

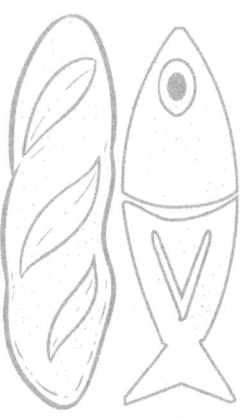

Stuffed and satisfied, the crowd relaxed as Jesus' disciples collected 12 baskets of leftovers. They stretched, yawned, and rested in the late afternoon sunshine. But their after-dinner conversation soon turned to Jesus – what kind of man was this? The people realized they had been in the presence of greatness. They had seen a first-class miracle. Not a one-off healing of a lone blind man or helping one lame person to walk. This was a big one. 5,000 beneficiaries experienced the wonder of Jesus' power.

In their struggle to make sense of the miracle they had experienced, they came to an amazing, yet inaccurate conclusion. John records the comments of the people. *After the people saw the miraculous sign that Jesus did, they began to say, "Surely this is the Prophet who is to come into the world"* (John 6:14). This was not just any prophet; the people knew *this one* was special. Moses had foretold a new and powerful prophet (Deuteronomy 18:15-19), and the people of Jesus' day seemed eager to identify this prophet as a forerunner of the Messiah (John 1:21).

Maybe Isaiah's words were swirling through their minds:

A voice of one calling: "In the desert prepare the way for the LORD; make straight in the wilderness a high-

way for our God. Every valley shall be raised up, every mountain and hill made low; the rough ground shall become level, the rugged places a plain. And the glory of the LORD will be revealed, and all mankind together will see it. For the mouth of the LORD has spoken." (Isaiah 40:3-5)

Malachi also wrote about the anticipated forerunner. *See, I will send my messenger, who will prepare the way before me* (Malachi 3:1a).

This Prophet was expected to usher in the long-awaited Messiah and prepare the nation for its coming Savior. The nation longed and hoped for The Prophet to initiate events leading to the entry of the Messiah. The well-fed 5,000 speculated that Jesus might be The Prophet. They realized that he was special, they just did not know *how special.*

Fascinatingly, they mistook Jesus for a prophet but not a priest.

In the Old Testament, two offices influenced the nation of Israel's religious life, *priests* and *prophets*. The kings had their roles to play as well, but that office focused on the military, economic, judicial, and political life of the country. The king had a spiritual role to play, but not to the degree of the priests and prophets. These two offices were on the front lines of the spiritual life of the nation.

The Role of the Priests

The job of the priest was rather routine – if you call killing sheep and cattle and burning their carcasses routine. Their job was to meet the ongoing religious requirements of the nation. And there were very clear standards for who could be a priest and who was excluded. There were many exclusions but three of the big ones were: family background, gender, and age. Priests were to come from

THE PRINCIPLE OF THE BIG BODY

the tribe of Levi and specifically from the family of Aaron. They were to be male. And they were to serve from the age of 25 (in some situations 30) to 50, after that they could serve as consultants.

> *The LORD said to Moses, "This applies to the Levites: Men twenty-five years old or more shall come to take part in the work at the Tent of Meeting, but at the age of fifty, they must retire from their regular service and work no longer. They may assist their brothers in performing their duties at the Tent of Meeting, but they themselves must not do the work. This, then, is how you are to assign the responsibilities of the Levites."* (Numbers 8:23-26)

The window for priestly service was quite restrictive, Levite (Aaronic) men, ages 25-50. The work was strenuous, especially at first, while they were setting up, taking down, and carrying the various components of the tabernacle and its furnishings. The daily, weekly, monthly, routine duties, along with festival sacrifices were laborious, gruesome tasks. Besides carrying the tabernacle, slaughtering animals, and burning their carcasses, the priests had other responsibilities. They taught the people the law of God (Ezra 7:10). They performed medical exams (Leviticus 13-15). They blew signal trumpets during times of danger and celebration (Numbers 10:1-10). And they led the people in musical worship (2 Chronicles 23:18). They probably also had a hand in weddings and funerals. The role of the priest would last as long as the nation. The work would go on and on.

The priests, however, were not always the *good guys*. Sometimes their work was rather perfunctory and lacked true spiritual vitality. And at times the priests were outright rebellious toward God. Aaron's sons, whether through a nonchalant or rebellious attitude, were burned to death when they presented *unauthorized fire* before the Lord (Leviticus 10:1-2). Eli's sons were involved in violence and immorality as they went about their priestly duties (1 Samuel 2:12-17, 22-36). Eli, his sons, and the entire nation paid for their wicked actions.

People did not surmise that Jesus might be a priest, but they did wonder if he was the long-awaited Prophet.

Role of the Prophets

Serving in parallel with the priests were the prophets. Beyond the routine, ongoing religious responsibilities, the nation of Israel had special challenges that called for a different form of spiritual guidance. This role was filled by the prophets.

Prophets came from a broad variety of backgrounds. Some started out as farmers (Amos 1:1 and 7:14-15) while others felt at home rubbing elbows with royalty. They represented many tribes and families. Men *and* women filled the role of prophet. And some, who were not killed along the way, served until they died in their old age. Prophets worked without the limiting restrictions placed upon the priests.

> *He functioned as a prophet, calling the spiritual leaders on the carpet for their lack of authentic faith and their self-serving application of biblical truth.*

Their work was hardly routine. There were schools to train prophets. Some only spoke, and some recorded their messages in writing. Their work was individualized and at times chaotic. They confronted godless rulers, proclaimed God's judgment, predicted restoration, preached to enemy capitals, and at times *rebuked corrupt priests*. The work of the prophets did not require a life-long commitment. They did their work, proclaimed God's message, confronted their adversaries, and then found an exit. Sometimes their work ended when their mission concluded, and sometimes they worked until their death.

These two offices plowed the same field. Neither was independent of the other, neither was better than the other. Some like Jeremiah and Ezekiel bridged the gap as they were both a priest and a prophet. The nation was at its best when priests and prophets each played their parts and played them well.

When Jesus finished feeding the 5,000, no one said, *wow – he must be a priest*! Feeding people on a grassy mountainside with a few fish and a few loaves of bread was not what priests did. Healing people of debilitating diseases and abnormalities was not what the priests did. The work Jesus did was outside the routine religious practices of the day. In fact, Jesus confronted the religious power structure and attacked the religious leaders. He functioned as a prophet, calling the spiritual leaders on the carpet for their lack of authentic faith and their self-serving application of biblical truth.

Jesus was easily classified among the prophets. While walking to Caesarea Philippi, he asked his disciples for an update on the rumors they had heard while in Bethsaida.

> *When Jesus came to the region of Caesarea Philippi, he asked his disciples, "Who do people say the Son of Man is?" They replied, "Some say John the Baptist; others say Elijah; and still others, Jeremiah or one of the prophets."* (Matthew 16:13-14)

The people never mistook Jesus for a priest, only a prophet.

Not Either or But Both
The writer of the Book of Hebrews complicates the picture. Just about the time we get comfortable thinking of Jesus as a prophet the writer describes Jesus as a great high priest!

> *Therefore, since we have a* **great high priest** *who has gone through the heavens, Jesus the Son of God, let us hold firmly to the faith we profess. For we do not have a* **high priest** *who is unable to sympathize with our weaknesses, but we have one who has been tempted in every way, just as we are--yet was without sin. Let us then approach the throne of grace with confidence, so that we may receive mercy and find grace to help us in our time of need.* (Hebrews 4:14-16)

So, which is he – a prophet or a priest? Fortunately for us, like Jeremiah and Ezekiel, he is both.

Jesus is comfortable working within the ongoing structure of our spiritual routines, meeting our ongoing needs for forgiveness and comfort. While at the same time, he easily operates in more open, unique, ambiguous environments. He is a great *high priest* and a powerful *prophet.*

Over the years, I have been dragged into discussion about Christian camping and its relationship with the local church. Three basic positions vie for supremacy. *First,* there are those who question the validity of any camp activity that is not under the authority of a *local church.* Some of their adherents fudge a little and approve of camps that exist to support the work of local churches. But they both tend to see camp ministry as the stepchild of the local church.

Second, pushing back are those who argue that camps exist to serve God's other great institution for structuring our world and shaping the next generation, the *family.* They hold that directly helping Christian families with their

THE PRINCIPLE OF THE BIG BODY

children's spiritual development, or influencing the entire family's spiritual life, is the best way to shape tomorrow's leaders. They contend that churches need to do what they do well and leave camp to those who know how to run camp.

Third, others argue that Christian churches and Christian families are all well and good, but camp is where non-Christians meet the Lord. They ask, If camps are tied too closely to local churches and only serve Christians, how then will we engage those outside the church, especially those who have a negative bias toward the church?

The discussion has value until it becomes a question of who is smarter, more in the right, or which position is most godly. Like many differences, everyone has some claim to being right, but everyone is wrong when it comes to being exclusively right.

In the Old Testament, the prophets were still under the authority of the priests. They were never granted the right to abandon the religious framework that God established. However, they were called to work outside that organizational structure. They were charged with being salt and light within the religious community.

> *Jesus is comfortable working within the ongoing structure of our spiritual routines, meeting our ongoing needs for forgiveness and comfort.*

Priestly responsibilities were well defined. They were not well suited for confronting political rulers, proclaiming judgment, performing miracles, leading missionary journeys, or rebuking the religious establishment. There were limits to the reach and effectiveness of both these religious roles. The priests needed the prophets, and the prophets needed the priests.

JESUS: CAMP DIRECTOR

Camp is a wonderful place where Jesus engages the physical and spiritual needs of people – lots of people. There are many ways to do camp and many good ways to have effective camp ministry. Some camps work well under the umbrella of a church or denomination. Other camps prosper as they connect with families from many churches and cities, blending a broad array of people for a week or weekend of synergy. And other camps have effective ministry as they reach into a lost world and introduce many young people to Christ for the very first time.

The body of Christ is a big body! Local churches, camps, schools, hospitals, mission agencies, radio stations, homeless shelters, and a host of other ministries each play a part. But the body of Christ is comprised of people – not institutions. We all need to connect within a local church, even while serving in camps and other parachurch ministries. In some ways the local church's responsibilities parallel the work of the Old Testament priests while parachurch functions look a little bit like their prophet counterparts.

Today, prophet-like, and priest-like roles continue to live with the dynamic tension and ambiguity that existed well before 5,000 well-fed people tried to classify Jesus as prophet. Those working in a prophet-like ministry need to recognize, appreciate, participate in, and support the work of their local church. Likewise, everyone in a priest-like role should thank God and honor those working in the prophet-like arenas of ministry. Turf wars have no place in Christian ministry. Jesus' ministry mirrored the work of prophets and priests. He lived a life that exemplified The *Principle of the Big Body* – and so much more.

THE PRINCIPLE OF THE BIG BODY

Discussion Questions

1. How would you describe your camp's relationship with local churches? Is it healthy and collaborative? Or is there tension and competition?

2. What partnerships does your camp have with local churches and like-minded ministries in your area? What more could you do to help each other minister more effectively?

3. Through your camp, what more can you do to honor local pastors and Christian leaders and support the churches and ministries in your area?

Personal Reflections

1. Are you actively involved in a local church? In what ways could you be more involved or supportive?

2. How do you think your pastor feels about your camp and your service there? Is it generally a positive or negative attitude?

3. Do you think you are more suited to minister as a priest or a prophet? Why do you think this is true?

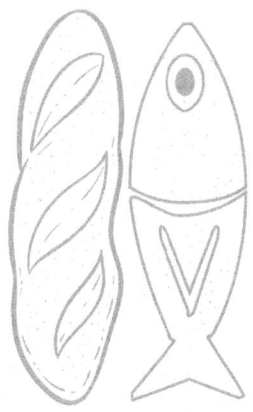

EPILOGUE

So, there you have them. In your hands are ten ministry principles I've drawn from the Feeding of the 5,000. Reflecting on this amazing miracle and ruminating on the way Jesus loved, served, taught, trained, and fed people, I am convinced that these simple principles can deepen and improve any ministry context.

As a camp guy, it is easy for me to see Jesus interacting with the people he cared for in a camp-like setting. But ministry takes place in a boatload of arenas, and these ten principles can enhance any church or parachurch institution that strives to do God's work in God's way.

In recognizing how Jesus ministered to others—his 12 interns and the 5,000 campers that came to camp that day—we see the perfect demonstration of love, servanthood, instruction, and care. Those of us involved in ministry, within Christian camping or beyond, should strive to apply these ten principles in the work God puts before us. The closer we come to imitating Jesus' methods of ministry, the more effective we will be.

My prayer is that these ten biblical principles of ministry will guide all of us, today and in the future, to learn from and model our lives after the greatest camp director of all time, Jesus!

ENDNOTES

[1] Ashley Denton, *Christian Outdoor Leadership*, (Fort Collins, Colorado, Smooth Stone Publishing, 2011) page 22.

[2] For a deeper discussion on the essential elements of Christian camping please see: Dan Bolin, *Blueprints*, Chapter 1: The Pillars of Camp, and Chapter 2: God's Revelation, (Arlington, Virginia, Refueling in Flight Publishing, 2022) pages 19-52.

[3] This account is found in John 1:44.

ACKNOWLEDGEMENTS

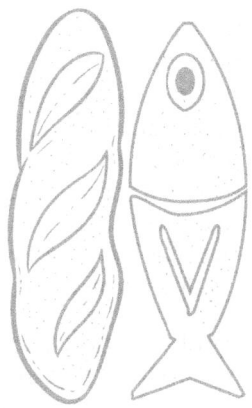

Many gifted people have made significant contributions to enhance and improve this project. *Jesus: Camp Director* has been a work in progress for a long time. To mention all the people who have invested in me, and this book, would ensure that some are omitted. However, a few who made major contributions are worthy of mention.

Ross Bay, Paul Biles, Brent Bounds, Wayne Braudrick, Dathan Brown, Dave Cairns, Joe Fahlman, Sharon Fraess, David Hartwig, Muhia Karianjahi, Susan Keiffer, April Moreton, Sue Nigh, Debra Pettit, Dan Smith, Kelly Starr, Evelyn Rivas Umana, and Scott Winn provided invaluable insights and improvements while the manuscript was emerging.

I am indebted to Ed McDowell for his kind and thoughtful foreword. (And to his faithful assistant, Sarah Eschbach, who graciously kept things on schedule.) This is a better project because of Ed's friendship and contribution.

The Refueling in Flight Board of Directors has heard me talk about this book for years and years. Their corporate and individual support, wisdom, and insights have polished this work and made it much better. Thank you to Cay Bolin, Bedford Holmes, Ken Sutterfield, and Brad Mercer.

My brother, Dr. Paul Bolin, was extremely gracious with his time, expertise, and encouragement. I now have much greater empathy for his former graduate students. Paul combed through the manuscript three times. Each pass uncovered more grammatical errors, poor word choices, mixed metaphors, and inarticulate ideas. I'm sure that additional examinations will reveal more pages that should be improved. Any misplaced commas or misspelled words are my responsibility alone.

Lori Price has worked for me (though not continuously) for about 30 years, at Pine Cove Camps, KVNE Radio, Christian Camping International, and now Refueling in Flight Ministries. Her technical skills, graphic design abilities, Christian camp experience, creative insights, and sheer tenacity have contributed enormously to this book.

My wife Cay has not only listened to me teach these ten principles for most of our 47 years of ministry together but has also provided a living example of their effectiveness.

To be clear, some illustrations have been modified to provide anonymity for those involved. However, I have attempted to retain the tone and emphasis of each event.

It is my prayer that this book will provide a complement to *Blueprints*. Whereas the earlier book focused on WHY Christian camping is so effective and examines God's design for this unique ministry, *Jesus: Camp Director* deals with the HOW of Christian camping and explores Jesus' methodology of ministry.

I hope that reading these pages on your own will provide new insights and affirm a host of ministry methods you are already practicing. But I also hope many camp leadership teams read this as groups. There are two sets of questions at the end of each chapter, one group is for personal reflection and the second collection is designed to stimulate group discussion.

Writing from an American perspective, this book may have words, illustrations, and concepts that are very Western. My hope is that each of these ten biblical principles will be adapted and applied to cultures around the world.

I welcome feedback and deeper discussion. Feel free to contact me at dan@danbolin.com.

JESUS: CAMP DIRECTOR

ABOUT THE AUTHOR

Dan Bolin worked 25 years at Pine Cove Christian Camps near Tyler, Texas, serving first as cabin counselor, then program director, children's camp director, and the final 14 years, as executive director. During that time, he spent 12 years on the Board of Directors of Christian Camp and Conference Association, two years as chair.

For more than a decade, Dan worked as a senior consultant for the Goehner Group training and equipping numerous camping leaders in the United States and Canada. Dan invested the final 11 years of his career as the International Director of Christian Camping International. Within that role he trained and encouraged Christian camping leaders in more than 30 countries.

Currently Dan is the President of Refueling in Flight Ministries, a Christian nonprofit organization designed to support his speaking, writing, and event leadership.

He has authored ten books and spoken at numerous ministry conferences. He writes a weekly devotional blog - Refueling in Flight - and teaches Outdoor Ministries courses in academic and practitioner contexts.

Dan and his wife, Cay, live outside Washington DC, near their daughter, son-in-law, and two delightful grandchildren.

JESUS: CAMP DIRECTOR

OTHER BOOKS BY THE AUTHOR

Jesus: Camp Director
5,000 Campers, 12 Interns, and 0 Kitchen Staff
RIF Publishing, 2023

Blueprints
Biblical Designs for Christian Camping: Yesterday, Today and Tomorrow
RIF Publishing, 2022

Fresh Bread
Self-Published, 2016

The Winning Run and Other Life Lessons from Baseball
with Ed Diaz | NavPress – 1999

A Hole in One and Other Life Lessons from Golf
NavPress – 1999

Avoiding the Blitz and Other Life Lessons from Football
NavPress – 1998

The One that Got Away and Other Life Lessons from Fishing
NavPress – 1998

How to Be Your Wife's Best Friend
with John Trent | NavPress – 1994

How to Be Your Little Man's Dad
with Ken Sutterfield | NavPress – 1993

How to Be Your Daughter's Daddy
NavPress – 1993

ABOUT REFUELING IN FLIGHT MINISTRIES

Refueling in Flight exists to encourage, assist, and connect Christian ministry leaders, especially camping leaders, in the United States and around the world. This is done through:

Writing
Weekly devotions, periodic blogs, and books

Teaching
Academic settings, professional training events, and churches

Connecting
CEO Dialogues, international partnerships, and retreats

To learn more about this ministry, visit: www.refuelinginflight.com

Scan to join the weekly email list for devotionals written by Dan Bolin.

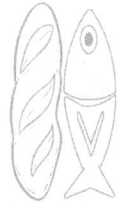

ABOUT ED MCDOWELL

Ed is the Executive Director of Warm Beach Camp Ministries. He also coaches and consults in the areas of Board Leadership and Development with the goal of bringing fresh perspective to perplexing situations.

Ed is the author of a devotional series titled *A Well Planted Faith in an Uprooted Culture*. The goal of his writing and speaking is to challenge people to have God's word inform the way they live.

Ed and his wife, Bev live on Camano Island, WA where they live out their life mission statement: To give our lives away for the cause of Jesus Christ to as many people as possible.

Made in the USA
Monee, IL
10 November 2023